D0385818

EVELYN WAUGH

Portrait of a Country Neighbour

Also by Frances Donaldson

FREDDY LONSDALE (1957)

CHILD OF THE TWENTIES (1962)

THE MARCONI SCANDAL (1962)

EVELYN WAUGH

Portrait of a Country Neighbour

FRANCES DONALDSON

Chilton Book Company

PHILADELPHIA NEW YORK LONDON

Published in the United States of America,
1968, by Chilton Book Company

Library of Congress Catalog Card Number 68–11545

Printed in Great Britain by Cox & Wyman Ltd,
London, Reading and Fakenham

TO LAURA

CONTENTS

ACKNOWLEDGEMENTS

I am grateful to the executors of the late Mr Evelyn Waugh for kindly allowing me to publish material which is in their copyright.

Photographs 7 and 8 were kindly found for me by Sir Michael Redgrave who took them himself; 13 is by Cecil Beaton; 6 is a post-card taken by Berekian of Nice and sent to me by Evelyn Waugh; 1 is by Yevonde for the Camera Press; 2 is by John Arthur; 3 comes from the Associated Press; 9 and 22 are by Karsh of Ottowa: 4, 5, and 10 come from the Radio Times Hulton Picture Library and 14, 15, 16, 17, 18, 19, 20 and 21 are by Mark Gerson.

The letter-head to the Piers Court writing-paper which decorates page 1 and can be seen in illustration 11 is by Reynolds Stone.

ILLUSTRATIONS

INTRODUCTION

In an impetuous article written for *The Spectator* soon after his father's death, entitled *Death in the Family* and inspired by filial piety, Auberon Waugh said several things that seem to me to need development.

He said that the obituaries in *The Sunday Times*, *The Times* and *The Tablet* were written by Christopher Sykes, Christopher Hollis and Douglas Woodruff, all friends of his father. 'All the others, whether laudatory or primly disapproving, had in common that they were written by people whose acquaintance with my father, if any, was of the very slightest.'

This is a fact that must have struck everyone who loved Evelyn, and struck them a blow. One or two of the people who wrote to the newspapers merely to record that, in some business dealing or on an occasion of meeting him, they had received an impression of courtesy or kindness seemed to do so because there was an obvious gap that needed to be filled. Most of the rest just turned a routine weekly penny in articles which pretended to knowledge they clearly had not got. But why were the pages left open for them? Where were the poets, the writers of the day?

Evelyn was so lavish, so unjealous with praise of any writer whose work he could approve. Young novelists of talent seldom appealed to him for words of introduction to the public without receiving an unexpectedly generous response, while faithfully over the years he took every opportunity to explain the claims of writers who had not found a wide public but whom he regarded as having exceptional merit. When he had failed to read a book at the time of its publication but later admired it, he went out of his way to ask some editor's permission to write a special article drawing attention to it. Accustomed himself in the latter part of his life to receiving only the most grudging praise, he never allowed this to influence his judgement. Anyone who knew him at home can testify that some of the happiest days of his life were those on which he received a book he could read with enjoyment, and he seldom failed to repay this with a public tribute to the writer. He was so enormously prejudiced that he missed much to admire in the works of the younger generations, but punctiliously, as a duty and a pleasure, he contributed all he could in critical appreciation to the art of which he was a master.

When a master dies surely that is the time for those who possess the gift of tongues to sing his praise. In this case the inexplicable omission was a wound not merely to those who loved him but also, I think, to the company of artists to whom he belonged. If Evelyn was to die so relatively unhonoured, who may any longer believe posterity will care more for him? Certainly one can say with absolute conviction that if Evelyn had outlived the few men he might reasonably have regarded as his peers, he would have been among the first to honour them.

One may guess at the reasons for the apparent carelessness. Many people no doubt refrained in modesty, believing the task would be undertaken by those closer to him, more able to do him justice. There is, after all, a presumption in writing about Evelyn which might deter all but the most insensitive pens; not so much because of his genius but because he was inimitable and inexplicable. His talent for the English language was at least as great in the spoken as in the written word. No writer trying to bring his personality to life on paper can do it by the apocryphal story, or the polished up version of half-forgotten phrases. (There are a certain number of anecdotes which go the rounds about him, but they have this in common that in each his exact words have been remembered.) The difficulty is not merely that in conversation he was capable of spontaneous, voluble, highly-talented speech but that his choice of the individual word was so singular and so unexpected. It has always been very noticeable that no one attempted parody. In the *New Statesman* competitions his name was often included in the lists of writers suggested for this purpose, but seldom chosen.

His son, in the article already referred to, has also said that the main point about his father was that he was 'simply the funniest man of his generation. He scarcely opened his mouth but to say something extremely funny. His house and life revolved round jokes'. Evelyn suffered from a melancholia of Johnsonian proportions, and he found life so terribly boring he could hardly endure from day to day; he was often ill, seldom completely well; he was the only person I have ever known who seemed sincerely to long for death; he was terrifying to a stranger, merciless to a friend; but it is true that his house and life revolved round jokes; very, very funny jokes.

It would not be surprising then if many people who might have written with understanding about him refrained from doing so in face of a self-confessed inability for the task.

But I surmise there is another reason why so many of the people who knew him failed to commemorate his death with written impressions of him as a man and a friend. In his youth he made for himself by his wit, his charm, his gaiety and his genius, a large circle of boon companions, many of whom were among the distinguished literary figures of the day. (In latter years he made few new friends.) But as he went through life, with a stroke of the pen here, a flick of the tongue there, he divested himself of many of the friends of his youth. He was born with the trick of hurting most devilishly with half a dozen words. It was not, or so I think, because so many of his friends no longer loved Evelyn that they could not write about him, but because they were unable to believe that he could – uselessly and without apparent regret – impale the friendship of a lifetime upon one heartless sentence if he any longer cared for them. One cannot assume the right publicly to mourn a man if one feels rejected by him.

But if the decimated company of his friends had not the heart to praise him, it was, nevertheless, not they who slowly built up the odious public image of him. This, as his son has said, was done by men who scarcely knew him.

INTRODUCTION

Evelyn's books and his personality were the result of a kind of dislocation of spirit so violent that, if he joins the small body of artists whose work survives their lifetime, he will forever be a subject of speculation for biographers and psychologists. But he was not the prim, stuffy, cross, snobbish, *little* man whose picture the journalists of the day have built up between them. Nothing in the public picture shows why, although he never numbered among his friends the craven or the sycophantic and in fact demanded some originality and social courage, to the end of his life so many people cared for him. Still less does it show the mixture of irresistible charm and dominance over other people which enabled him, when he cared to do so, to recall to his side even those he had estranged most deeply. His faults were fair game for anyone who chose to write about him, but few have ever portrayed his extraordinary qualities. Evelyn was touched by genius, a thing infinitely hard to pin down, but apparent in almost everything he did, everything he said.

His biographer will be confronted with the usual difficulty in writing the life of a literary man: the work, which speaks best for itself, was performed in relatively uneventful circumstances. No momentous Cabinet decisions, no historic battles, no discoveries to change the course of humanity; in the main simply the life of an ordinary citizen. In Evelyn's case there are a few good fights on record and a quite exceptional number of letters which, because he made so great a name so early, have been assiduously preserved over the years. These letters will, when collected together and published, do more than any other writer can to reflect his wit, originality and charm, the small change of his daily life, since so many of them were written to while away the time and to further his inveterate appetite for gossip. They are witty and capricious and essentially trivial; but they bear the marks of his immense erudition, the imprint of his talent. The difficulty for the biographer who writes today will be that, for reasons of kindness and taste rather than from fear of libel, so many of his letters are likely to be unpublishable. And the limitation of letters is that, although they may reveal more than the writer is aware, they still remain within confines of his own choosing. If the truth about so complex a personality is to be left for posterity it can only be from a composite, many-sided picture contributed to by those who knew him.

I have reflected long on this point because there is one circumstance which made my own knowledge of him almost unique among people living today – I knew him at home, as part of a family. Few have ever been able to say the same and of these – notable among them Monsignor Ronald Knox – some have died before him.

I will not protest, as is the fashion, my inadequacy for a self-imposed task. I have never found such protestations on the part of other writers very convincing and as a rule they are the prelude to an inadequate book. The humility I feel is towards Evelyn, and, if it is an impertinence for me to write about him, no one else can absolve me from it. I merely hope by relying on memory to make a small contribution.

INTRODUCTION

The apology I owe to readers is that my memories are slender. No one but a Boswell who had sat beside him over the years with pen and paper could bring Evelyn to life again, but I might have played the part. I have a good memory for speech and I had the opportunity. But I was too lazy then and I cannot now repair the omission. I cannot invent, embellish or polish up my recollections, and the only claim I can make for a thin narrative, small clues and slight facts, is that I have not tried to do so. This is an impression: not an ambitious work but simply an attempt to show Evelyn as I knew him in his own home.

PART ONE

PIERS COURT

Chapter 1

FIRST LOVE

We went to live in the Gloucestershire Cotswolds in the autumn of 1947. At that time it was a very backward part of the country, an outlandish empire of the Duke of Beaufort. The news that we were members of the Socialist Party had preceded us and effectively closed to us all but three or four doors. It thus happened that the few people we did know belonged to the more sophisticated elements of society, people who lived in London as well as Gloucestershire, or for one reason or another were among the more enlightened. None of them, however, knew the Waughs. One or two had had an encounter with Evelyn because at an earlier date he had put his house up for sale, although failing to get the price he had hoped for he had withdrawn it. People who had gone to see it had found the manner with which he said 'My wife will show you the house', and the ostentatious speed with which he vanished up the stairs or into the garden offensive and slightly ludicrous. All of them would have liked to meet him, but they had no great ambition when they found this not reciprocated, and they faintly resented feeling reproved for overtures they had not made. One of our new friends, a man of strong social proclivity, flushed when we mentioned Evelyn's name and said: 'Ah! but he goes a bit far.' Months later when I asked Evelyn to account for the flush, he said that this man had developed the habit of dropping in without invitation or warning and had taken his weekend guests to Piers Court for entertainment, as one might to a church or a famous house open to the public.

We believed that sooner or later we should meet the Waughs, because we moved, as far as Jack and I could be said at that time to move at all, on the edges of overlapping social worlds. Simon Elwes, hearing we had gone to live near them, asked me once if we knew them and I replied that we didn't and that I didn't particularly want to.

'He sounds too frightening,' I said. 'So ruthless, and I'm not good at that kind of conversation.'

'I know what you mean,' Simon said. He reflected a moment and then he said: 'Most people when they find their friends have some little weakness rather like them for it, find it human and endearing. But *not Evelyn . . .*'

We lived in Gloucestershire for six months without hearing anything more than this of the Waughs and without meeting them. But it was not true that we did not want to meet them. One would always like to know the more distinguished of the people living near. Then one day in the early spring, my Nanny having gone to London leaving me to look after not merely my own child but also hers, I was standing in the farmyard dressed in jeans and feeling harassed and dirty, when a car drove in and a fair-haired young woman got out of it. She walked towards me and held out her hand.

'My name is Laura Waugh,' she said.

'Oh!' I replied. 'Are you Mrs Evelyn Waugh?'

She said that she was. She had come to pay a formal call and to ask us to go on a day later in the week to their house for a drink. She said that Andrea Cowdin had told them we were living near. Andrea is an American and a great friend of my father who was then still alive. She had a house in Los Angeles and when Evelyn went to supervise the attempt which proved abortive to make a film of *Brideshead Revisited* the Waughs had stayed in her house. Laura's call lasted about half an hour and we walked to a point from which I could show her the farm. She had a small farm of her own and we talked about the friends we had in common and about Ayrshire cows. When she was leaving I said:

'Well, we'll come for a drink on Thursday.'

'Oh!' she replied. 'Won't you come for dinner?'

And I thought with amusement as well as pleasure that I had come through some test. Laura was boldly backing her judgement.

That night I spoke to Andrea on the telephone about something else.

'By the way,' I said, 'Mrs Evelyn Waugh called on us today.'

There was a moment's silence and then Andrea burst out laughing.

'But I only saw him at lunch time yesterday,' she said, 'and he didn't go down till late last night. She must have gone off the first second she could.'

Andrea said, I remember, that Evelyn had asked her to stay, but as she was in London for only a few days she had refused. He had said that owing to the rationing of food they would be unable to honour her in the way they would like: 'But we could boil the baby.'

In the spring of 1948 people dining out in the country did not dress for dinner. In the first place petrol was rationed and, although there was a small allowance for private use, most people muddled up the coupons allocated for pleasure with those for business, and would just as soon not be wearing evening dress if stopped by the police. Secondly, coal was also rationed and most houses were too cold.

When I was dressing to go to the Waughs on that first evening Jack came into my room.

'What are you going to wear?' he asked.

'I am going to wear an equivocal dress that might be either,' I replied, 'but I think you should wear a dinner-jacket. She didn't say "Don't change", and I think it safer.'

Jack agreed. Always afterwards we believed that if we had decided otherwise we would have spent an evening of petrified interchange with our hosts and never met them again. For Evelyn to change for dinner was, like brushing your teeth or hair, an everyday necessity. His attitude was not that of the pukka sahib and I don't think he would have changed on safari with the lions roaming round. But the habit of not changing was, like socialism and modern architecture, one of the reasons for his attachment to the past. If we had entered his room clean and tidy but in day dress, his mood would instantly have set against us. Evelyn chose the people he wanted to know; and, if the apparently inconsequent conditions with which he hedged round his friendship prevented him from knowing nine-tenths of the most interesting people in the world, it was a fact of which he remained in invincible ignorance. He was incapable of calculation in small matters of personal taste. For this reason he occasionally broke his own rules.

Laura had told us the way to Piers Court but we had trouble in finding it in the dark. Presently our headlights shone on a white wooden paling on the side of what looked like a drive. Venturing a little further we saw two red brick gate pillars which supported stone urns of a distinguished, faintly rakish elegance. They did not look as though they had started life at this relatively plain gateway, and they announced without equivocation that this was the house of the eccentric personality with whom we were going to dine.

At that time Evelyn was in his late forties and he still seemed young. He used to take a cure once a year of a stiffish kind prescribed by a Dr Goller and he also went for very long walks. He kept entirely to the road but he often covered eight or nine miles.

He looked very small, but not fat and unexpectedly attractive. I think he wore a velvet dinner-jacket. He spoke in the light, faintly fruity voice I always thought one of his greatest charms. From the moment we entered the room everything went very easily. He talked to me of my father.

Although I did not know it until later on he was curious to meet me on account of my father, Freddy Lonsdale, a playwright. When the Waughs stayed with Andrea Cowdin in Los Angeles Freddy had been in the house. But they scarcely saw him. The reason for this was that Freddy, in his own way quite as odd as Evelyn, was determined not to meet them. A person of great talent, he instinctively knew that Evelyn's talents were greater, and, totally uneducated, he also knew that Evelyn was highly educated and as far as he was concerned incomprehensible. I am not suggesting that he analysed and understood this, or that in his thoughts he was so complimentary to Evelyn. He merely felt that he didn't want to meet him. So, as long as the Waughs were in the house, he had his meals sent to him in his room and pretended to be working. He was never seen except as a vague shadow in the passages. Simon Elwes painted a picture of the Waughs with Andrea and some other people sitting in her garden in which Freddy can be seen standing some distance away at the side. This unusual conduct was of irresistible interest to Evelyn and made him hopeful and curious about me.

Then he established Jack's antecedents. Was he not a contemporary of Tom Mitford, a friend of Emerald Cunard? During all this time we drank rather a lot. Evelyn always served short drinks in very large glasses. One sherry or gin with something or other in his house was the equivalent of about three anywhere else. Some years after this he bought some glasses in France and had them engraved with the words *In Vino Caritas*, but they were delicate and Laura put them away because so many got broken.

I always loved the drawing-room at Piers Court. The rest of the house was a question of taste – Evelyn's taste. Personally I became very fond of that too, but I could understand why other people disliked it. Evelyn liked dark surfaces and patterns, heavy furniture, silver and glass. There was much that was Victorian in the house but his taste was masculine and, although the house was enlivened with personal eccentricities, it was genuinely of the period, not, as so much Victoriana is today, faintly pansy in flavour, amusing rather than worthy. In his library the carved shelves were built out in bays as they are in a public library and painted dark green, but it was a big room and the effect was rather beautiful while this arrangement provided room for his collection of books. The dining-room was sombre but the hall, staircase and landing above were light and elegant. The whole house right down to the Abyssinian paintings in the gentlemen's lavatory was uniquely different from any other house I have ever been in.

The drawing-room into which we were shown on that first night spoke as much of Laura as of Evelyn. They both loved and had considerable knowledge of fine furniture and they bought eighteenth-century pieces when they could afford to. On the walls hung pictures from Evelyn's collection of Victorian painters including the Augustus Egg of two girls in a boat, and I remember with vivid affection the faded green velvet curtains banded with chintz which hung in the circular bay window and the cushions which they had bought in a country house sale. On this night a fire burned in the grate and the chintz-covered chairs and sofa were reassuring. So was Evelyn's manner, warm and hospitable, the reverse of frightening.

In mood he was always very mercurial. I have often gone into a room where he sat slumped in a chair, ill and melancholy, beyond the power of speech: 'My wife will entertain you,' he would mutter.

Five minutes later if one had the luck to make some remark to Laura which interested him he would rise in his chair, take command of the conversation and race into the mood of fun and jokes. He had an immensely dominating personality and one's spirits rose and fell with his.

On this first night, although we did not yet understand him, it was clear he was in good spirits. By halfway through dinner the first fine flush of love was on us and Evelyn had embarked on the life history of Maundy Gregory.

Maundy Gregory was a man who at the time Lloyd George was liberally handing out peerages acquired some means of knowing in advance the list of intended honours. His practice was to visit men whom he knew were to receive a knighthood or a peerage and, saying that he had influence in the matter, suggest that in return for a fairly large sum of money he might be able to secure something for them. In this way he accumulated a fortune while the money paid to him always seemed to have been well spent. This part of the story might have been invented by Evelyn; the rest undoubtedly was.

He said that Maundy Gregory had murdered his wife by administering strong doses of arsenic. There then followed a scene in a London restaurant which I have completely forgotten in which by a series of stupid statements Gregory aroused suspicion. But the part of the story on which Evelyn mainly exercised his powers of invention concerned Maundy Gregory's efforts to remove the traces of arsenic from the body. He believed that to do this it was necessary to keep it in water. He therefore propped his dead wife beside him in his sports car and drove round the graveyards bordering the Thames until he found one that was known to become submerged in winter. Here he interviewed the vicar and explained that his wife had just died and had always expressed a romantic desire to be buried in a place where water could wash over her. The vicar, moved by this simple wish and possibly gratified by appreciation of his normally unpopular graveyard, agreed to bury Mrs Gregory but asked which undertakers he should consult about the committal. Maundy Gregory then replied that it so happened his wife was with him in the car outside, and suggested the vicar should take over all the arrangements.

I have forgotten the end of this story and I am not sure I have got it quite right, but it went roughly like this. When Evelyn told a story he gesticulated with his hands and face and there was a slight gurgle in his voice which I suppose one might term a chuckle although in his case it was a mere ripple. He had an expostulatory air of relish of the preposterous antics of other people. That night he embroidered his invention as he went, employing his gifts for ribaldry and the macabre, his astonishing command of language. It seemed to us that his performance was in no way inferior to the best of his writing, but no Boswell could have saved it for posterity; I doubt if the next morning he could have done so himself.

When we left his house that first evening he accompanied us through the hall to the door.

'Don't,' he implored us, '*don't* just come once and then never come again.'

The second time I went to Piers Court was in the morning. I called to deliver something we had promised to lend, a book or a catalogue. Evelyn was away but the butler, Elwood, smiled when he opened the door and insisted on fetching Laura. I was pleased because butlers always know the status of guests in the house and act accordingly, and by now I was half in love with this whole household. Laura came to the door and asked me whether I would like to see her small farm and we wandered round it. She had twenty-five acres and a small milking herd. Evelyn always said: 'My wife has a little peasant holding,' and he alleged that it lost more than they could afford. Laura's farm supplied the house with milk, cream, butter and eggs, but more important than this to the economy, the farm labour was responsible for the whole of the garden and kitchen garden. Evelyn always ignored this fact when he balanced the books. Laura had an old servant of her own family who ran the farm, whose name I think was Saunders. He looked at her with eyes of love and treated her as might some old nanny. He learned to disapprove of Jack and me because when we went together to Ayrshire sales we would not let Laura pay too much for the cows she bid for. We sometimes came home empty-handed and he regarded this as a disgrace and a humiliation to the family. I know not why but I suppose he thought it *infra dig* not to be able to afford something you had shown you wanted.

As we walked round the farm I asked Laura if Evelyn was often as funny as he had been on the night we dined and she replied sometimes, but only when he was happy. She said that it was an embarrassment to her not to be able to ask her neighbours to the house in the ordinary way, but it had been more of an embarrassment when she had done so. The last time she had asked some people to tea, she said Evelyn had risen about five o'clock in the afternoon and saying a formal good-bye had said that he must go and take a bath. He could never stand even short periods of active boredom, and when he went to a play which he did not enjoy he would roll about and groan in his seat.

When we dined for the second time at the Waughs', Evelyn had spent the intervening time in London and there he had gathered some information. Arriving back he punctually invited us to dine and received us with all honours. But when we sat down to dinner he faced us most solemnly.

'Is it true,' he asked, 'is it true what Laura and I have been told? Are you Socialists?'

Modestly Jack replied that we were. Not very active ones, possibly rather pink ones, but Socialists, fully paid-up members of the Labour Party.

For eighteen years Jack and I have believed that when a few seconds later he dropped the subject and turned to other things he swallowed a rule that he would in no circumstances meet members of the Labour Party. Frank Pakenham (now Longford) and Tom Driberg were friends made in his youth before the formulation of his prejudices. Frank is also a Roman Catholic while Mr Driberg was of special interest to him. But, if asked, I would have said that to my certain knowledge he absolutely refused to meet any other Socialist until, late in life, he met and very much liked Hugh Gaitskell. However, when lately I discussed this matter with Laura, she said that all of this was nonsense. It had so happened that on the one or two occasions we had tried to bring Socialists into his life they had been people he did not want to know for other reasons, and he had invented this rule to prevent us. Laura gave me chapter and verse for this statement and I was forced to believe her.

So here is a salutory lesson – if one is needed – for anyone writing or reading about Evelyn. No one except Laura had any idea what he was really like behind the personality he had built for himself, and he cared so little what one believed. Most people desire rather strongly that the truth about themselves as they see it shall be known. 'I may be stupid, but I really have not got that kind of rigid outlook.' Evelyn invented this fiction (in the cause of good manners?

Evelyn as he was when I first knew him

The outside of Piers Court

Evelyn and Laura arriving from New York the year we met

in order to tease?) rather than state the harmless truth that he did not want to meet someone.

However, even if there were no pig-headed rule to be broken, one cannot support the idea that other people's politics were of absolute indifference to him. He disliked politicians, and impartially held both parties in complete contempt, refusing to treat either as a topic for serious conversation. While the 1945 Labour Government was in power I asked him once whether he thought it right that the Mother Superior of the Convent she attended should tell his daughter it was not a sin to cheat the railways.

'It's an occupied country ...' he replied. 'It may be Teresa's duty to rob the railways.'

But when I congratulated him on the Conservative victory at the polls, saying that now things might become more as he liked them, he said fiercely:

'The Conservative Party have never put the clock back a single second.'

Nevertheless, he deeply hated liberalism, as all his published works proclaim, and I still believe that if we had not first breached the defences in disguise, as it were, we should have found Piers Court closed to us. If, as is now said, he had no objection in principle to Socialists, it is most likely that this was because he wished to avoid giving credence to the idea that he supported the Conservative Party.

Chapter 2

SOCIAL OCCASIONS

So, between his prejudices and his inability to enjoy ordinary society, Evelyn was very much cut off. And yet he pined for human company. Because of this Laura had come so quickly to visit us and because of this he tried to persuade me to have cards printed, so that I might accompany her on subsequent forays. He would plan excitedly for weeks to meet someone about whom he had heard something which interested him, and he loved to entertain people he liked. Once in 1948 we took Laura to a musical festival at Cheltenham, an hour's drive away. We had arranged to go back to supper with Evelyn and when we got there about eleven o'clock at night we told him we had seen Eddie Sackville West.

'Did you ask him to supper?' Evelyn asked Laura, and with a sigh to Jack on his way to wash, 'Poor Laura. She has no social sense.'

When new people arrived in the district I used to ask them for a drink to meet the Waughs. I can remember no single instance of introducing anyone new into his life with great success. The first time Freddy, my father, came to stay we took him to dine. Evelyn seemed very anxious to meet him and I did not yet know about the Los Angeles incident, although I did sense that Freddy was not pleased that I had arranged to go to the Waughs'. The meeting was a civilized but noticeable failure. Both these men earned their living by wit, both were relished by their friends because they were so amusing in conversation. Neither could discover a grain of humour in the other. If asked both would have confessed to finding the other a bore. Not for the first time I noticed that humour, always considered the great ameliorator, can divide as completely as it unites.

Freddy was at a great disadvantage because Evelyn, who in his own house led the conversation, lived on a different plane of cultural taste and knowledge. He had a disconcerting habit of saying: 'As you know from the works of So-and-So . . .', mentioning some little-read authority, and then pausing slightly. If you nodded agreement, it was apparent you lied, if you said unfortunately you had not read the works, you interrupted the flow of his conversation. I solved the difficulty early by shaking my head but saying nothing. Freddy, by a force of character as strong as Evelyn's, survived two dinners, and there was an occasion when the two met alone in New York which was said to have been a success. Personally I always believed that if this were so it was largely because they both drank themselves into a stupor. In any case Freddy refused any longer to go to Piers Court when he stayed with us.

But there was nothing unusual in the failure of these two to find anything to say to each other. When we were known to have made friends with the Waughs many of our other friends wished to meet them, but they seldom wished to twice. I must emphasise the fact that this was not because Evelyn behaved badly or did not strive to please. Away from his own home he was acquiring a reputation for unpredictable bad manners, but he sat up too late in London and drank too much, while he could never stand the strain of periods as long as a weekend. When he came to our house or we took people to his for a drink, he would arrive in the room full of hope and curiosity and exert himself to amuse. But so often his jokes fell by the way, were not recognized as jokes. Sometimes there was a brutal truth behind them which in conversation shocked people, so that although they might find his books very funny they did not find him funny at all; chiefly they were so stylized that one needed some previous knowledge of him or his world to catch them as they passed. But he had the faculty of pulverising other people, reducing them to silence. He told me once that he had been reproved by a priest for saying that someone was a bore. When he protested that it was a minor criticism, the priest replied that nine people out of ten did not recognize a bore when they met one, but, once a man had been labelled, then everyone found him boring. But what after all is a bore? One thing that makes even the most interesting people boring is to feel profoundly uneasy. I have seen intelligent and worldly men simply unable to answer Evelyn when he asked them some ordinary question.

He was set apart not merely by his talents but by an exceptional brain and by his encyclopaedic knowledge of all the things that interested him. His views on politics or current affairs were so strangely different from other people's that they made no basis for conversation, but quite reasonably he had no wish to discuss books, or plays, or architecture, or painting in everyday cocktail-party style. He could not bear to have his own works praised to his face as a gambit of opening conversation. All over America earnest women provoked grunts and groans by long-winded expressions of their admiration for his novels, and in England his manner prohibited this choice of topic. The professionalism of the writer is seldom sufficiently understood, and people who would not dream of discussing his technique with a painter make nothing of artlessly dissecting the work of a novelist. I remember once Evelyn told me that a woman friend of his had spoken to him in praise of my prose style, and there was something in his manner suggesting amusement which put me on the defensive.

'I hope you weren't beastly about it,' I said.

'Oh no,' he replied in shocked tones. 'I was only amused at the poor beast thinking she knows one prose style from another.'

So what was there left to talk about? The conversation that on light occasions entertained Evelyn most concerned the whims, peculiarities or doings of people. He was endlessly curious about this. If his interest had been broadly based, had extended to the everyday affairs of every man, if his conversation had been informed by sympathy, gravity and wisdom, this would have been found endearing and completely comprehensible – a benevolent and human characteristic in the great man. People were after all his stock in trade, the material in which he worked. Unfortunately he confined his interest to a very small circle and he had a preference for the absurd over the heroic. Evelyn, I fear, was a gossip.

It was his extremely narrow vision of the human race that made so many social occasions such a flop. Evelyn liked the smarter of the intellectuals, the more intellectual of the smart – no one else. No one else liked him. With all the more ordinary people of the world, but also with three-quarters of the most interesting, he was unable to establish any communication. This was the fact – impossible to explain, useless to excuse. His predilection for gossip had something to do with it, however, since as a basis for conversation gossip is viable only within a small circle.

His exclusiveness gave the lie to the public image of him as a crassly silly snob. I remember one journalist who wrote of him as 'dining with Bert', and 'staying with Andrew', or names to that effect. But this concept was wholly false. It was not merely that he was extremely formal in tone, anything but a name dropper; he chose his society as rigorously in one group as in another. He had a romantic attachment to the aristocratic virtues, but he had no use for those of the aristocracy who lacked these. He liked high spirits, extreme confidence, social ease, the rich, the beautiful and the brave – and these only for short periods. Three-parts misanthropic, one part gregarious and highly curious, he was inclined to like women better than men because they prattle easily.

But the weakness in attributing any particular quality to Evelyn is that he could not allow anyone to dictate his attitude or virtues to him. Consequently, if he was accused of some quality usually regarded as contemptible, where other men would be aroused to shame or hypocrisy, he studied it, polished up his performance, and, treating it as both normal and admirable, made it his own. By the end of his life, as he has made plain in *The Ordeal of Gilbert Pinfold* and as is obvious in some of the letters which form a later chapter of this book, he was parodying himself. Consequently, it was never any good looking straight at him to learn the truth about him.

When one asks whether a man is a snob one may mean either is he more snobbish than the rest of us, or, is his snobbishness predominant over his other qualities? If the question is put in the second way, Evelyn, as I have already said, comes through with flying colours. His aggressiveness, his exclusiveness and his terror of boredom were far stronger than his snobbishness. But, put in the first way, there are two pieces of evidence against him. The first was this inability to communicate with anyone who did not belong by birth or education and training to that very small world which, loose and conglomerate, still regards itself as the upper class.

Secondly, damning evidence is to be found in his work. So sure, so dry, so brilliant in delineating character from all the spheres of life about which, convicted on the first count, he should have known nothing – Mrs Leonard in the war trilogy, Sarum Smith, Frank de Souza, dozens of others in his imaginary army – as soon as he writes of the upper classes he betrays a soft centre. Mr Crouchback (the father), his ideal of goodness and purity, a sentimental creation whose counterpart has never been seen on earth and whose sanctity is ultimately based on a horrible family pride; Ivor Claire, both in his glory, riding his horse with the 'intent face of a pianist', and in his shame; Julia Stitch with her compendious oceans who restores Guy to health with a cry of '*C'è scapato il Capitano*'; all these stray into his pages from another world created by another novelist. Curiously enough it is Evelyn himself who points out to us where, refined by wit and decked out in new glories of language, they come from. In *Unconditional Surrender* Everard Spruce, talking to his secretaries, Frankie and Coney, of the death of Virginia Troy, says she was the last of twenty years' succession of heroines – 'the ghosts of romance who walked between the two wars'. Then he reads from a novel a passage describing the type, and he says:

'I bet neither of you know who wrote that. You'll say Michael Arlen.'

In the *Spectator* article Evelyn's son says: 'My father's life was largely spent in the avoidance of boredom and of people who were likely to bore him.' The irony of Evelyn's life was that he won the struggle against bores but was himself overwhelmed by boredom. In *The Ordeal of Gilbert Pinfold* referring to the saying: 'It is later than you think', he remarks that it was never later than Mr Pinfold thought. This, like the whole of the section in which it occurs, is clearly autobiographical. He struggled every day just to get through the day.

When we first knew him he strove against this paralysing boredom in odd ways. He went, as I have said, for walks over very long distances. Twice a week he spent the afternoon in the cinema in Dursley, irrespective, I think, of the film that was showing, once for each change of programme. He entertained himself with grandiose projects in his garden. He built what became known as The Edifice – a semi-circular stone wall about ten feet in height, surmounted with battlements and with a paved area beneath it. When this was finished he advertised for human skulls to adorn the battlements. He received a surprising number of replies, which I doubt if he had expected, and he had to refuse most of the offerings. The Edifice was not a great success. Many people thought it hideous and Evelyn himself was not satisfied with it although he got pleasure from the building. A path in the garden was made by inverting and planting empty champagne bottles, and he constantly brought home pieces of sculpture for the garden. Later he designed and had made two iron gates which he erected nearer the house than the gates with the urns which we noticed on our first visit, and outside these he placed the now famous notice NO ADMITTANCE ON BUSINESS.

This notice viewed with so much surprise and amusement by people who did not know him expressed something very real in his nature. He resented not merely the attentions of commercial travellers but any unannounced invasion of his privacy, and his taste for ceremony here supported a fierce intention to guard himself against intrusion. I remember calling on him once in the evening when Laura was away. I was expected but when I rang the bell I got no reply. After ringing once or twice more I opened the door and ventured into the hall. As I did this Evelyn appeared.

'Ah!' he said. 'Caught you.'

This remark was made with the greatest good temper. He was alone and pleased to see me. Nevertheless, it reflected his spontaneous feeling that it was improper for anyone to open the door of his house and walk in.

Every morning he read *The Times* from cover to cover, taking particular interest both in the Law Reports and the advertisements. In the evenings he did the crossword puzzle. The day of the week on which he received the *New Statesman* became known as Black Friday because it always provoked him so much. Once he could endure it no more and he cancelled it, but Friday became so much blacker without it that he had to order it again. I think he read it until the end of his life because in the autumn of 1964 he told me Friday had become very dull now that the *New Statesman* had nothing but praise for the Government.

But the chief occupation of the morning was letter-writing. He never had a secretary and he answered all his letters by hand. He had an enormous correspondence for two reasons. He refused to use the telephone so that all those small matters about which other people speak to each other were dealt with by post-card. Secondly, the post kept him informed of the movements of that part of society which interested him. He had two or three regular correspondents, all of whom I think were women, to whom he wrote and from whom he received regular bulletins. They were carefully chosen both for their talent for letter-writing and for their knowledge of London society. When his favourite gossip left to live in Paris, he appointed a London successor. In writing letters he whiled away the morning, in receiving them he served one of his major interests.

Because he enjoyed gossip he raised it to the status of a minor art. On his regular if infrequent visits to London he usually came home with a number of stories so singular and so improbable that when we first knew him we put them down to his own powers of invention. We soon learned that even if they had been improved upon they were invariably founded on fact. He was always first with the news because he educated his friends to collect and recount the smallest doings of the people in whom he was interested. One learned to give weight to the most trivial happenings and relish to the smallest absurdities.

Once, describing someone to him, I said:

'He is rather reticent. That's a good quality, don't you think?'

'Oh, no,' Evelyn said. 'A beastly quality.'

'Do you really think that?'

'Certainly,' he replied. 'Absolutely necessary in one's family, but beastly in anyone else.'

But he was never a mischievous gossip. He liked the news simply for its own sake, and I know of no single instance where he did damage by repeating malicious remarks to the person concerned. Intent on damage, he used direct means.

I have a postcard from him – undated – which perfectly illustrates his methods.

Brownell x Blair last Wed in hospital.
D. Astor gave bride luncheon leaving groom.
Rev. Brain protestant vicar St Pancras
officiated. Not asked to luncheon.

This means that George Orwell whose real name was Blair (we were known to admire his works) and whom we had met for the first and last time a few weeks earlier when Evelyn took us to visit him in a hospital on the hills above Stroud – had on the previous Wednesday married Miss Sonia Brownell who worked with Mr Cyril Connolly on the magazine *Horizon*. The detail is an example of the art of making bricks without straw.

But on looking through the letters we received from him at that time I am reminded that equally he could be highly mysterious for no obvious reason. A letter written on cheap paper which has lines to guide the writer, a gold band round it and a picture of the Virgin and Child, reads:

August 30th

Dear Frankie,

The editress of 'Contact' of 7 Cork Street, W.1 has

written to me (why?) to ask if you will write her 2,000 words for £20 on the life of a farmer – I presume she means a lady of fashion who leaves Mayfair for the stye – 'not at all lyrical' she says 'but rather revealing if possible'. Will you let her know direct if you will or not?

Yours ever
Evelyn

I have further correspondence with him on this matter because there was some doubt in my mind as to the time of payment for the article, but he at no point supplied the answer to the question 'why', bracketed in this first letter, which, as I discovered later for myself, was that the editress of *Contact* was Miss Clarissa Churchill, the present Lady Avon, a great friend of his.

Chapter 3

A FAMILY FRIENDSHIP

THERE were two questions which, once it was known that Jack and I knew Evelyn well, people invariably asked us – with different degrees of frankness, with more or less grace. One was, how can you like him so much? The other was: why does he like you? Even now that he is dead people still ask: how did it happen you knew him so well?

The answer to the first question depends so much on the fact implicit in the second, that I must try to explain that.

Neither smart nor intellectual, by accidents of birth and upbringing we occupied a kind of no-man's-land between the two. He sent Laura to call on us because he knew my father; we passed muster at dinner because we knew some of his friends and enough of some others to enter lightly into the spirit of his conversation (nothing unusual here, the discovery of friends in common is a most sought-after basis for conversation between acquaintances); and because, unlike many people, we laughed uproariously at his jokes.

How did we manage to live beside him for so long in amity? Evelyn himself was aware that here was a matter for speculation. He used ruefully to refer to us as 'My only friends'. The copy we have of *Officers and Gentlemen* is inscribed in his handwriting:

A FAMILY FRIENDSHIP

For Jack and Frankie
(My only friends)
With love
Evelyn

We lived in amity just because we lived so near to him. In the country two families often strike up friendships of a very close kind, dining often together, developing the same interests, calling upon each other in times of melancholy or trouble. Jack and I made close friends not merely with Evelyn but also with Laura, while our children made friends with theirs. Family relationships such as this ensure a good deal of tolerance. It was not so much that we never quarrelled with Evelyn as that we could afford to do so.

On occasion he was very angry with us. I remember once we were just about to set off to Piers Court for dinner where they had other people staying, when we discovered that our whole herd of cows was loose in a wheatfield. Flushed and flustered and full of apologies we arrived about half an hour late, to find the whole company waiting and to be met with extreme displeasure. I sat next to Evelyn at dinner and receiving the brunt of his mood, became in my turn equally displeased. If, when we left that night, we had driven out of the centre of his life, he would forever have shaken his head censoriously when Jack's name was mentioned, and muttered: 'A man who prefers his cows to his friends.' But the next time he was bored and melancholy Laura telephoned to ask us to go and entertain him, and I, still angry with Evelyn, could not resist

Laura's invitation because she was quite innocent of offence.

But we did not often quarrel with him and the pleasures of his company were far greater than the pain. He was full of contradictions but the strangest of all was that, in spite of the *accidie* and the boredom, he had such enormous zest. This quality which was very apparent when he was in a good mood is also to be found in his work and distinguishes it from the flatly pessimistic satire of many of his contemporaries.

He was far easier (or so one gathers from the stories that are told) in his own home than away. He used to go regularly to London, if only for a day or two at a time. As a rule he had business with his agent or publisher, but at lunch time he made for White's Club where he sat drinking with the inmates until it was time to view some Victorian picture in one of the many galleries round St James's Street, or stagger off to the Stroud train and home. When he dined in London people used to tell us that he drank too much and made himself a nuisance. He himself said that he spent a fortune sending flowers in the morning to women he was told he had offended in the evening. He was ebullient and aggressive. Sometimes he meant to be rude, but often he was surprised to find his conversation had been taken amiss. But, as far as one could tell, although he sent the flowers, he was never seriously disturbed. He thought it a pity other people were so silly. And he enjoyed well-taken reprisals. Once Jack travelled down on a crowded train with him about five o'clock in the evening after he had spent the day at White's. Evelyn was bustling

The sitting-room at Piers Court

The library at Piers Court

Evelyn and Laura in Cannes. A post-card on the back of which he wrote 'Hat by Donaldson' (*See page 44*)

(*Below*)

Evelyn posing and Simon Elwes at work on his painting (*See page 8*) Photographs taken by Sir Michael Redgrave

and pushing along the train to find a seat when a stranger turned and said:

'Don't be a brute, sir.'

He was delighted and this became a family term of rebuke.

But if further reason is wanted why he should have liked us, it may have been because we adored him. Laura once remarked to him that it had been horrid of him to be unkind to someone or other, 'because', she said, 'he loves you.'

'Nonsense,' Evelyn replied. 'I know who loves me.'

And he did know exactly. He was, in matters that concerned himself, the most perceptive man I ever knew. He knew not merely who loved him, but who loved his jokes and his work, who was charmed by his personality and his poses. Like most people who have much to give, he demanded in return appreciation, but unlike so many other people, he hated adulation. To please him it was necessary to laugh spontaneously and at the right moment, while if one wished to speak of his work one had to make some particular and pointed comment. Anything else he turned off sternly and coldly, so that one felt guilty not so much of an impertinence as of a thoroughly boring conversational gambit. I think of all his qualities this was the most unusual. There is a saying that every man can be bought if one can discover his price. In my experience almost every man can be flattered if one can discover the strength at which the balm may be safely applied. Not Evelyn. One could not treat him casually or without the deference his talents deserved, but the deference had to be felt, the appreciation had to be real. It had also to be instinct in one's manner, not considered or in any way underlined.

Nowadays it is often said that conversation is dead. No one could say that who had met Evelyn. It was a marvellous pleasure simply to sit and listen to him. It was not merely his control of an exuberant flow of language that gave this pleasure; by the unexpectedness of his thought and phraseology he could impart freshness to all the most ordinary and overworked words.

He had one or two small tricks of speech. He said: 'I suppose,' with a sigh, or 'I expect'. He did not pronounce the words differently from anyone else, but by dropping the 'so' he made it sound as though he had. He said: 'It was very rum' where other people say 'odd' or 'peculiar', and he used the expression 'poor beast' not with a savage inflexion but with the mixture of ridicule and pity with which he normally regarded humanity.

He was enormously educative. He widened and extended our interest in all the things which interested him. He collected books, pictures, lithographs, and, in a small way as we all do, furniture. On the morning when there was a country house sale in the district, or a visit planned to an '*antiquaire*' he arrived looking hopeful and perky as when embarking on a holiday. He loved the architecture of every age except the twentieth century.

He continually lent us books from his library. His taste in literature was very certain, if limited by his prejudices, and just as he genuinely disliked flattery, so he seemed completely without jealousy of other writers. Among writers he introduced to us before the public learned to appreciate their work were Anthony Powell, Muriel Spark and Sybille Bedford.

He was extremely generous with his books and on the only occasion when I seriously damaged a book of his, by dropping it in the mud as I got out of the car, he was surprisingly forgiving. But when he failed to find some book he wanted he invariably accused us of having it, whether or not it was one we had borrowed. This is a difficult thing to explain because these accusations were in essence a joke, and taken as a joke, but he pursued them with deadly seriousness. On one occasion he believed or affected to believe that we had filched his copy of *A Question of Upbringing* by Anthony Powell. Without ever being unpleasant about it he always spoke as though it was a fact that we had failed to return this book. For instance we still have a piece of paper which accompanied a book he returned to us on which is written:

> I hope that this act of reparation makes you feel guilty about the rape of A. Powell CBE.

We seem to have succumbed to pressure on this occasion because when Evelyn died Laura found in his library two copies of *A Question of Upbringing* and one of them has on the back of the binding Jack's bookplate and on the paper facing it Evelyn's, while the second one has only Evelyn's. And yet, and yet . . . When, after Laura returned it to us, I remarked to Jack that this was a first edition of Anthony

Powell carrying Evelyn's bookplate and therefore an object of value, he looked at it and discovered that it was a second edition; while the book which has since that time resided in our library and which I had assumed we bought to replace the copy given to Evelyn is a first edition. This is a piece of evidence which points in both directions as does also the unexplained fact that between us we had three copies. Now we shall never know, but Evelyn certainly would have put a very definite construction on these facts.

One other matter in connection with books must be recorded. Whenever he lent us books he invariably included among them some piece of special pleading in the form of a work on the Christian religion. These books became of great interest to Jack and, together with many conversations, had the result, not entirely acceptable to Evelyn, of returning him to the Protestant faith of his fathers.

Evelyn never discussed writing or writers with us at length, but he used to say odd little things about them. He said he owed a great debt to the distressed clergy because in the days of his youth publishers used to employ the classical scholars among them to read proofs. It was from them he said he had learned grammar and punctuation. One cannot avoid clichés in so well-worn a language, he said, in answer to a question, but one should not lead up to them. Once I asked him whether he enjoyed Henry James and he replied:

'Yes, of course. But it's very rum that he never seemed to know what his characters did when he wasn't there.'

And when Jack asked him if he had ever got into trouble for basing the characters in a novel too closely on some living person, he said:

'I've never been horsewhipped on the steps of my club, if that's what you mean.'

The only time I have ever known him speak of a novel he was writing was when he was at work on *Men at Arms*. Jack asked him how it was going, and he said: 'A little differently from how I intended. There is a character called Apthorpe who has got the bit between his teeth.'

And he killed Apthorpe off at the end of the first volume because he wanted no more of him.

It was known to us that his first novel *Decline and Fall* was to some extent based on experience as for a short period in his youth he had been a schoolmaster. One evening at dinner Jack asked him whether he had enjoyed this part of his life. He said it had been all right, but he had got the sack.

'The trouble,' he said, 'was the daylight saving.'

He explained that it had been his practice to go down to the local pub in the evening after his day's work was over and there to replenish his spirits after the fatigues of the day. He used to slip into the school after the boys had gone to bed and pass unnoticed up the stairs to his room. One night, following his usual custom, he had found the staircase thronged with boys in their pyjamas and dressing-gowns.

'Ooh, sir,' their young voices rang out in the hush that followed his entrance, 'are you all right, sir.' 'Ooh, sir, can I help you, sir.' 'Let me give you my arm, sir.'

The next morning the headmaster had sent for him and given him the sack.

Evelyn was an extremely generous host and in all the years we knew him he was always very kind and affectionate to Jack and me. Almost every letter we have from him either from Piers Court or Combe Florey ends 'Come soon', and when we went he always behaved as though we did him a kindness. He always produced his best wine for us, often a bottle of something special.

He did not do that for everyone. In the early years when we first knew them the Waughs used often to have people to stay for the weekend. This was a highly dangerous procedure, because Evelyn who looked forward excitedly to the visit all the week before, could seldom endure anyone for so long a period. Laura used to invite us to dinner on the second evening by which time she expected to need outside help. On one of these occasions Evelyn was waiting for us on the steps of the front door, and, as Jack got out of the car, he took him by the arm and walked him down the drive talking earnestly. I had been driving the car and I got out a second or two later; as I did so I heard Evelyn say:

'But the claret is all right.'

'Oh Evelyn,' I said, shocked. 'Has it come to that?'

He turned to me.

'A base character,' he said.

Elwood, the butler, had instructions to serve at dinner a fairly moderate champagne without offering an alternative.

Evelyn had just advised Jack to refuse this. Claret would be taken round second. What actually happened was that Elwood, misunderstanding his instructions, offered Evelyn and Jack the claret the first time round so that Evelyn, almost speechless with rage, had to direct him to offer it as an alternative to us all.

But I would not give the impression that he often treated his house-guests badly, although his temperament made long visits hazardous. He was extremely hospitable by nature and on this occasion he had been seriously tried.

Evelyn was very fond of wine and in a small way a connoisseur. For many years of his life he drank claret at luncheon and also at dinner. But there came a time when he lost his taste for claret and sold the whole of his cellar, some of it to us, and ever after drank burgundy. Jack used to get his wine from the Wine Society, and, possibly because it was cheaper than buying from a wine merchant or because some wine Jack had appealed to him, Evelyn bought a certain amount of wine on Jack's account. This led to several letters on the subject. The first which is perfectly serious I give because wine is a matter that interests so many people. It is undated and written from White's Club.

Dear Jack

Of the cheaper clarets the Laujac seems to me to be the best. It will be better later.

The Talbot 43 is delicious and will improve.

The Talbot 37 as you remember is fine.

The sherry is good.

Cockburn's 'Ripened in wood' is the best of the ports.

I am not happy about all the money you paid for my drinking. We must get together behind Frankie's back and settle up.

Meanwhile will you please order me 5 dozen of each Talbot and of the Laujac. Two dozen sherry. Two dozen Cockburns 181– port.

Laura is in radiant health. Not so myself who have been behaving as though I was twenty years younger than I am with disastrous results. Well I ought to know better than to go boating in fancy dress with the young married set.

Evelyn

The full title of the Society from which Jack bought the wine is The International Exhibition Co-operative Wine Society and it was formed to buy up surplus stocks after the closing of the great Exhibition of 1851 at the Crystal Palace. Evelyn enjoyed treating it as a modern type of co-operative of socialist inspiration and this accounts for the two following communications Jack received from him. These are written in a childish handwriting in red ink on post-cards and on each a hammer and sickle is drawn and painted with the red ink. The signature is chosen because Anthony Crosland was at that time Labour MP for South Gloucestershire, the constituency in which we lived, and was known to be a friend of ours.

DERE KOMRADE THEM COOPS AS DUN US DIRT AGAIN. ONLY 4 DOZ. WE PADE FER 5. I MEAN TER SY A RAKE OFFS A RAKOV BUT THIS IS A BIT MUTCH EH CROSSLAND.

Evelyn standing in his library

Evelyn beside the Glastonbury bowl (*See page 115*)

Piers Court
Stinchcombe Nr Dursley Glos.

Oct 29th 1954

My Dear Frankie

What a very charming birthday present! Where did you find it? I am entirely captivated. Thank you with all my heart.

Yours ever

Evelyn

Please give my love to Freda

Station: Berkeley Road.

From Mr. EVELYN WAUGH, Piers Court, Nr. Dursley, Glos. Dursley 2150.

DERE KOMRADE THEM COOPS AS DUN US DIRT AGAIN. ONLY 4 DOZ. WE PADE FER 5. I MEAN TER SY A RAKE OFFS A RAKOV BUT THIS IS A BIT MUTCH EH CROSSLAND

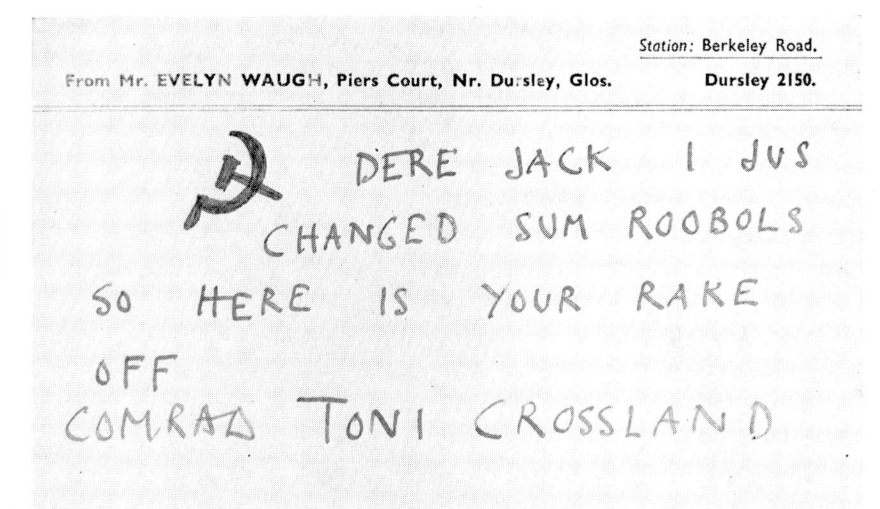

Station: Berkeley Road.

From Mr. EVELYN WAUGH, Piers Court, Nr. Dursley, Glos. Dursley 2150.

DERE JACK I JUS CHANGED SUM ROOBOLS SO HERE IS YOUR RAKE OFF

COMRAD TONI CROSSLAND

Two post-cards

(*opposite*) A letter

The Cecil Beaton photograph used by Nancy Spain (*See pages 87–8*)

And:

DERE JACK I JUS CHANGED SUM ROOBOLS SO HERE IS YOUR RAKE OFF. COMRAD TONI CROSSLAND.

A third question which people often asked us was: 'What is he like with his children?' and in the mind's eye of the questioner one could see the pale brood shut away in the tower with their lesson books for company. But in fact Evelyn was much beloved by children who, although they found him rather terrifying, appreciated his quality. He was very much the Victorian papa, and used to say 'Out, out, out' to the little ones when they came into the room unasked, and shoo them away. But they were quite used to this and disliked it no more than any other method of telling them they could not do as they wanted.

Once when Jack and I arrived at Piers Court on a summer's evening we met Evelyn coming in from the garden. He told us that Hatty, then a very small child, had come into his library and said:

'Papa, there are a lot of small animals in the garden. Do come and see them.'

'What kind of animals?' he asked.

'Small, white animals with horns.'

'Calves,' Evelyn suggested.

'No, no, Papa. Very small animals.'

'Sheep?'

'No, no, Papa. Very small, white animals with horns.'

Following her to a corner of the garden Evelyn had seen a cloud of Cabbage White butterflies hovering over a flower-bed.

As the children grew old enough to have meals in the dining-room they were taught that civilized conversation was expected of them.

'What have you young people got to tell us to entertain us?' he used to say. And while talking to the one who sat next to him, he instructed the others to talk to each other. He preferred female children and intelligent ones and these responded to his treatment as to a rather delightful challenge. Alice Jolliffe was his favourite and he used to say that, if anything happened to Laura, he should marry her when she grew up. 'Sweet Alice', he said, when talking of her to his children, or 'your future stepmother'. There was a room at the back of Piers Court that was approached by outside steps. Laura gave this to the children to make into a playroom and they were busy furnishing it one day when Evelyn looked in.

'Ah!' he said. 'What you need is a green table to write poetry at.' And rushing back into the house he fetched them one.

When he motored round the countryside in company with his children he taught them to recite benedictions or maledictions to his neighbours as he passed their houses. One of these owned a factory that made rubber goods and Evelyn insisted on regarding him as responsible for the control of birth throughout the country. Imprecations greeted his house, but as the car drove on to the house of his next door neighbour, more admired (at a distance), the refrain changed to the words of the 122nd Psalm.

'God bless Colonel Brown. They shall prosper that love

him. Peace be within his walls and prosperity within his palaces.'

Having read *Work Suspended*, I said to him:

'You have a gift for fathers. You seem to be fond of them.' He replied: 'Yes, quite right. It is a role in which I rather like to see myself.'

Recently I asked my elder daughter, Rose, whether it was true, as we had always thought, that as children they were not afraid of Evelyn, but on the contrary regarded him with pleasure.

'Oh, yes,' she replied. 'And of course all that talking at meals was very useful when we first grew up. All the same,' she added, 'Joanna and I used to resent being made to feel absolutely barbaric because we wore short dresses at dinner.'

It seems that Rose and Joanna Talbot, when aged fourteen to sixteen, used to go to dinner in the kind of short dresses their mothers thought appropriate to girls of that age, and were unfairly put to shame by the Waugh children who swept down in long, crazy grandeur from the dressing-up box.

But as his children grew up Evelyn relaxed none of his attitudes or standards for them or their friends. He expected them to dress and cut their hair as he had in his youth and he made no allowances for the passing of time or the lesser affluence of the young. This led to a rather strange kind of University rag. Some Oxford undergraduates who were friends of his daughter Teresa – then at Somerville – wrote to Evelyn asking him to go to Oxford to address them. If he would accept their invitation they wrote they would be glad if he would join them afterwards in 'some sort of a meal'. Evelyn replied tersely that, as he did not care to partake of 'some sort of a meal', he could not accept their invitation. This angered the young who had written in humility and, if he had accepted their invitation, would have stretched their resources to entertain him. They plotted a curious rebuke.

Two young men drove in a car from Oxford to Piers Court. Arrived there it seems probable they lost their nerve. They deposited on the doorstep a large swan, plucked and dressed ready for the oven, which, history relates, had been residing in a deep freeze in Oxford for several years. Evelyn, unwilling to enter into the spirit of the letter of invitation, entered with zest into the spirit of a rag. Laura in her turn issued an invitation. Jack and I were away at the time. But when we got back we found a message awaiting us asking us to dinner on a date which had already passed to eat a swan. I telephoned to Laura to ask for an explanation.

'Did you eat it?' I asked after listening to what she said. And she replied that they had.

'It was perfectly edible,' she said in reply to a further question. 'Not very interesting.'

Meal-times at Piers Court were always very ceremonial. The heavy Victorian furniture was resplendent with highly-polished silver and glass. A carved wooden lion (acquired we think in Abyssinia) stood in front of the fireplace and also a musical box which was made to work by turning the handle. As each of the children grew old enough to appear in the dining-room he or she took over from an elder the task of turning the handle as the guests took their places at meals. It was impossible to discover whether this attention was designed to please or embarrass, but if the latter it normally succeeded. I wondered whether Evelyn awarded marks to his guests for the conversation that broke the silence following the grinding out of the tune. Again when one of the children greeted the arrival of some unusual guest at dinner, such as a visitor from America, with a long, laudatory speech which had clearly been carefully composed and rehearsed, it was difficult to decide whether it should be accepted as an honour or resented as a tease. But in spite of the attention given by Evelyn to the ceremonies of the dining-room he was never quite satisfied because of small lapses of Laura's. Meals were nearly always eaten to the accompaniment of sighing complaints: 'Laura, shouldn't there be two salt cellars when there are more than four people?' or 'sponge cakes with gooseberry fool?' and so on. And it was true that Laura, who had no aim other than to please Evelyn, was not always able to do so because of certain idiosyncrasies of her own character. During the whole of one winter, the ceremonial, the beautifully served meals and the sighing complaints took place to the accompaniment of slight thuds against the floor beneath and in an atmosphere of a very faint but decidedly obnoxious smell. Laura, becoming short of space in her farm buildings, had placed her hens on deep litter in the cellar under the dining-room. Again it was a great source of joy to Jack and me when, later at Combe Florey, without any diminution of the ritual, the Italian manservant who had been engaged for the house but proved to be a genius with cows, served dinner dressed in grey flannel trousers and a pullover.

The food itself was invariably excellent, both when they had a cook and later when Laura did most of the cooking herself. Evelyn, however, always maintained that it was practically uneatable. Many of the letters we have from him are on this subject. A box of cigars or some wine would arrive with apologies 'for the execrable dinner', and here is a characteristic letter thanking us for a present:

Saturday in the Octave of the
Assumption 1954

Dear Jack and Frankie,

The cheese arrived like a parachute load in a siege or seige I think the former perhaps. I was literally very very hungry and in despair. I began on it at once with my children sobbing, but unsatisfied, around me. Thank you. Thank you. I need not fear the horrors of the dining-room for weeks now.

Yours ever
Evelyn

While our son Thomas was at Eton, Teresa Waugh was at the convent at Ascot next door. On one occasion in 1950 it was arranged that Evelyn and I should go together and take the two of them out. Shortly before this Evelyn had expressed a wish for a straw boater and Jack had found him one and sent it to him as a present. ('It is a lovely hat,' he wrote, 'not reasonable but I wear it with pyjamas in the first bitter half hour of the day and it cheers me up.') Making the arrangements for our visit Evelyn sent Thomas a postcard modelled on those printed forms that make it easy for soldiers to write home. The small print in the following represents Evelyn's handwriting on the postcard, the lines and the large print were written by Thomas in reply.

> I {can / ~~cannot~~} lunch on Saturday June 17th
>
> Please meet me at OLD HOUSE HOTEL, WINDSOR.
>
> Please wear a {~~black coke~~ / ~~grey coke~~ / boater}
>
> The Castle is {open / ~~shut~~} that afternoon.
>
> Signed. THOMAS DONALDSON.

We set off together driven by Mr Prothero from the garage at Stinchcombe who always drove Evelyn when Laura was not present. Evelyn was very fond of this gentleman but he deplored his clothes which consisted of a tweed coat and a cap. He had wished to give him a chauffeur's coat and cap for a Christmas present but Laura had absolutely forbidden it. The morning passed quite ordinarily except that, as Teresa got into the car, Evelyn remarked to her that the voluble nun who had opened the door to him and whom he apparently knew, had been 'drinking again'.

Luncheon too passed without incident except that

Evelyn's face wore an air of apology which suggested controlled discomfort. After luncheon matters improved because we went to St George's Chapel and he always enjoyed sight-seeing. My memory records two incidents. One, when Teresa discovered the tomb of Henry VIII, and, turning to Evelyn, said:

'Is that . . .?'

'Yes,' he replied. 'You may spit on that.'

The other was when we joined for a while the crowd behind a guide conducting a tour round the chapel. This guide stood on a tombstone and explained that every member of the Royal family when he died is first buried here. After six months the remains are disinterred and taken elsewhere for permanent burial. He pointed to his feet.

'The Duke of Kent's down there now,' he said, his familiarity with death and with royalty producing a macabre effect reminiscent of Evelyn himself.

When we left St George's Teresa got on the box of one of the hackney cabs that in those days amused tourists at Windsor (the driver happening to be absent) and picked up the reins with the intention of driving it away. Thomas, nervous of his reputation at Eton, began to implore her to get down but Evelyn looked on with pride and said nothing. Thomas's pleas at length won the day, but Evelyn would not have prevented her and, when Thomas also refused to go down a street that was out-of-bounds, he remarked to me that he had no idea Eton taught boys to be so conventional.

Afterwards we had tea in Fuller's. I had been against this because I thought the teashop at Eton more suitable, but the children preferred the cakes at Fuller's and Evelyn said he was absolutely unable to walk back to Eton. He looked incredibly funny sitting red in the face and bolt upright among the cake-eating women and children. But it was not until after we had dropped Teresa that I realized how much he had suffered. He simply collapsed in the corner of the car and when Mr Prothero stopped at the nearest hotel he could scarcely walk to the table where we consumed, in unequal proportions, a bottle of champagne. He revived just sufficiently to drive to another hotel where we had dinner and more champagne and where he was offended by the waiter, who, assuming he was drunk, asked: 'Are you all right, sir?' During dinner he explained to me to which school, club, regiment or sport each of our fellow guests was affiliated or addicted. He had a collector's knowledge of ties.

On the way home we had to stop twice more, and, as Evelyn regarded it as undignified to tell Mr Prothero and the waiters in the hotels the real reason for these calls, we on both occasions consumed further quantities of alcohol, one visit thus leading to another and bringing us home very tipsy.

Then there was the fête. This was of some importance because it received publicity and fostered the ridiculous notion that Evelyn had retired to the country to play the part of the 'Squire', thus cutting himself off from the 'literary life' of his time and neglecting to nourish his talent. The 'Squire' in fiction and usually in life is a benevolently patronising figure, sitting on the Bench, dispensing hospitality, setting an example by going to the village church on Sundays. If Evelyn is to be seen in terms of a cliché, he was much more the old, darkling lord, brooding glumly in his library, too misanthropic to know his neighbours, too eccentric to take part in the life of the county. But as it happens none of this bears any relation to fact. Evelyn lived in the country because if he had lived in London he would not merely have neglected to nourish his talent, he would have been dead before he was fifty. He was a very reckless character, and what with trotting off to White's every day, and gossiping with friends and quarrelling with foes, he would have had no literary life at all. He lived in the country as an act of self-preservation. Also it has to be said that in his house at one time or another we met Graham Greene, Henry Green, Ronald Knox, Anthony Powell, L. P. Hartley, Christopher Sykes, Cyril Connolly, Christopher Hollis; while I know from his conversation that he numbered among his friends or acquaintances practically every writer of his age. It is difficult to see from whom he cut himself off except the journalists who invented these fictions, and even then, as I shall show, not always these.

The fête was really Laura's. She conceived the idea of raising money for St Dominic's Roman Catholic Church, Dursley by holding this party in her garden. But, as Evelyn watched her preparations, he became appalled by what he regarded as the incompetence of her arrangements, the paucity of the entertainment she proposed to offer. And so he took it over, merely to save his poor wife from public discredit.

Once he had involved himself he became very excited about it, and so did we all, and he decided to open his house to the public to show them his collection of nineteenth-century lithographs, his library of books and manuscripts and his collection of pictures. He conscripted the children for various jobs and to my daughter Rose he gave the part of acting as guide to those people who wished to view his pictures. He rehearsed her very carefully in what she was to say and on the afternoon of the fête her childish voice was to be heard, echoing innocently through his house, voicing remarks of his invention. The effect was remarkably funny and a great success with everyone. I had supposed that here at least her young memory would be able to supply me with some real detail, but of all that afternoon the wretched girl remembers only this.

William Douglas Home had telephoned and asked in very civil terms whether he might come to the fête and write a story about it for the *Sunday Express*, and Evelyn had given him permission. Rose, in describing a pair of pictures, one representing a serious young man with a serious girl regarding an open book on a table, the other a dandified young man, lolling at a window with a different kind of girl, was instructed to say:

'This one is reading for honours – this one for a pluck. The newspaper that can be seen in the pocket of the second one is a kind of rag, the equivalent of, one might say, today's *Sunday Express*.' – a tease for William Douglas Home.

But her performance was more distinguished than her memory, and Evelyn gave her for it the gown of a Doctor of Literature which he had received with an honorary degree from some overseas university, and Pugin's *Contrasts*.

When Jack and I arrived at the fête we found that two young Americans had chosen to present themselves in the hope of an interview. They had been rather roughly pressed into service, and were at that moment moving furniture. Later one of them was sent with Jack to act as car park attendant while the other was added to the troop of children performing various menial jobs. They seemed very young and rather baffled by their reception, but when they returned to their own country one of them wrote what is said to be an exceedingly funny article describing the fête, and it was this as much as anything that gave the impression it was representative of the life Evelyn had adopted.

But the most memorable of all the things connected with this day was the performance of the Poor Clares. The fête took place during one of those long patches of rainy weather which so often occur in July, and Evelyn took the precaution of sending some money to the Poor Clares with a request that they would pray for good weather. All the morning it rained and rained until twenty minutes before the fête was due to begin. Then the sun appeared and remained in a blue sky until the last of the visitors had left. As we retired into the house to give drinks to the local band, the downpour began again.

Lunching alone with Evelyn and Laura one day I told them that I had the night before listened to Lord Beaverbrook speaking on the wireless.

'What did he say?' one of them asked.

I replied that he had been rather self-pitying, dwelling on his age.

' "I am a man with a past," he said, "I have no future." '

'*He's* got a future,' Evelyn observed grimly.

Once we went on holiday to Belgium with Laura and Evelyn. When we returned more than one person looked at us with great curiosity and said: 'Didn't you quarrel?' But Evelyn on holiday was at his best, brimming over with excitement and pleasure like a child, although on this occasion it was rather spoiled because he was ill when we got to Bruges.

We had arranged to meet at Victoria station and when we got there he was already ensconced in a seat in a Pullman carriage, looking absolutely absurd, his round, happy face crowned by a tweed cap. In *Work Suspended* the narrator, when he has to sell up his father's house and has nowhere to live, is bothered to know what to do with his hats.

> I owned what now seemed a multitude of them, of one sort and another; two of them silk – the tall hat I took to weddings and a second I had bought some years earlier when I thought for a time that I was going to take to fox-hunting; there were a bowler, a panama, a black, a brown and a grey soft hat, a green hat from Salzburg, a

sombrero, some tweed caps for use on board ship and in trains – all these had accumulated from time to time and all, with the possible exception of the sombrero, were more or less indispensable.

It may not be generally known that at some period in Evelyn's youth he thought for a time he was going to take to fox-hunting. He did take to it for a little while and he also frequented the establishment of a character famous in the twenties called Colonel Hance, who taught riding to the *jeunesse dorée* and owed his success with them to the fact that he cursed them like a sergeant-major with a company of troopers. One of Evelyn's characteristics was that he was physically fearless – he regarded courage not as a good but as a necessary quality – and he used to look back on his riding days with nostalgic pride.

'Some tweed caps for use on board ship or in trains.' On the rack above Evelyn's head when we travelled together there was a bowler. When we arrived at Dover he took off the tweed cap and put on the bowler to go through the customs. Once on board ship he changed to the tweed cap again. In these small ways he got all he could out of the delightful adventure of being away from home.

When we had arrived at Ostend and collected the luggage together, Evelyn began to explain in French to the porter where we wanted it to go. He spoke French like Winston Churchill only less fluently, and presently I said to him:

'Evelyn, he probably speaks perfectly good English.'

'Oh yes,' he replied, 'but we mustn't encourage him.'

We spent only two or three days together because in Brussels we separated, the Waughs going to stay with friends. We visited all the usual sights, but only two incidents remain now in my memory.

On the first night at Ostend we went to the casino so that Laura might gamble. We walked home to the hotel and we completely lost our way. It was late and quite dark and we had no idea where we were. Evelyn went alone down a side street and resourceful as ever chose a house in which the light was on and where there was a doctor's plate. He rang the bell and when the door opened, he could be heard saying:

'*Pardonnez-moi. Nous sommes perdus . . .*'

Without any further encouragement the doctor came out and directed us in English how to find our hotel.

In Bruges we were all four together in a picture gallery, but Evelyn had wandered on in front of us. Presently he came trotting back.

'A splendid likeness of Cyril in the next room,' he said.

We hurried through and began to look with care at those of the pictures that were portraits, but after some time we all gave it up in despair.

Evelyn pointed to a large seascape. From the top right hand corner a small fish swam towards the centre of the canvas. It had an undeniable look of Mr Connolly.

Chapter 4

THE REAL MR PINFOLD

WE were present on the periphery of the events on which Evelyn founded *The Ordeal of Gilbert Pinfold*. When I first read this novel I noticed that it differed in many respects from what I cannot help regarding as the real story. Since the major events took place in Evelyn's mind there is for that part of it no real story, but there was, nevertheless, a sequence of actual events leading up to and away from the period of mental disturbance which he described in the book, and secondly there was the version he told himself at the time. There were also some details of his recovery recounted by Laura in his presence, with which he did not argue. When I read *Pinfold* I was disappointed because in my view the version he gave there was less interesting and less amusing than the story as we knew it. From that day until after I had written this account I had not re-read the novel and, although I could remember what he left out of the book, I could not be sure what he put in. I propose here, in the interests of an eye-witness account, to describe the events as I remember them regardless of the fact that some parts of my story have been wonderfully better told by Evelyn himself.

Insomnia is the writer's occupational distress. Sometimes

it is caused by the over-stimulated mind racing at night and preventing the onset of sleep. More often the busy subconscious, never at rest, brutally awakens the sleeper in the unrefreshed hours of the early morning. There seems to be no natural method of preventing the premature awakening. Fresh air and exercise may bring a few hours sleep, but, once the body is slightly restored, the brain jerks into life again. In purely physical terms it may be possible to live on a few hours sleep every night, but few people, least of all the imaginative, have the mental endurance to stand for weeks at a stretch the slow passage of time between three or four o'clock in the morning and the arrival of day. The regular use of sleeping drugs is very common among writers.

Evelyn suffered permanently and terribly from insomnia. He strove against this affliction in many ways. At one time for quite a long period he used to get up in the early hours and shave. He said that his smooth face on the smooth pillow induced sleep. But in the main he had to rely on drugs, and, since in matters that concerned himself he was completely reckless, as he acquired resistance he increased the dose.

He employed in those days – it would not be accurate to say he was attended by, because he seldom saw him – a doctor whose practice was in a neighbouring town, and whom he referred to as 'My Medical Adviser', conversationally the 'MA'. The MA was a nervous man who at that time had great troubles of his own. He was terrified of Evelyn as was another local doctor who attended the children and who had once been reproved for entering the house by opening the door and walking in when he had failed to get an immediate answer to the bell. These things may or may not account for the fact that Evelyn was able to acquire unlimited quantities of a sleeping draught containing bromide and chloral. I am almost sure he had more than one source of supply.

In the winter of 1955 he suffered from pain, diagnosed, I believe, as rheumatism, and he was unusually ill and melancholy. He resorted to the bromide and chloral as a pain-killer by day as well as a sleep-inducer by night, and over a period of about six weeks he absorbed poisonously large quantities. Then after Christmas he departed, as he invariably did at this time of year, on his travels. On this occasion he took ship for Colombo. It throws a light on subsequent events and on Evelyn's character that he left the bromide and chloral behind him.

A week or so after he left, Laura came to our house and told us she was horribly worried about him. She asked for our word that what she was about to say would go no further, and then for Jack's help. She said that Evelyn had seemed very ill and melancholy when he left, but that, since with every day he spent at home he became worse, she had let him go, believing that nothing but the change would cure him. She then read to us selected parts of several letters she had received from him. In these letters he said that travelling on the ship with him there was a party of 'existentialists' who had perfected a form of long-range telepathy. For some reason of which he was not aware, he had incurred their hostility and they were using their unusual gift to persecute him. It had begun by his being plagued by the sound of his name in the air and, at night when he went to bed, by half-heard conversations in which his name constantly occurred and which seemed at first to come from the next door cabin. Soon he was allowed no respite from these voices by day or night and he was quite unable to sleep. The last of the letters was written from a hotel in Cairo and said that he had left the ship and intended to continue his journey over land in order to escape from his enemies. It was this letter which brought Laura to see us. Evelyn said that he had had twenty-four hours peace in the hotel in Cairo but on the second day the voices had mockingly resumed their continuous conversation and their extraordinary power seemed in no way diminished through separation by miles of ocean. He referred to a neighbour who believed in the ministration of 'the Box' – a matter which had earned his amusement and scorn – and said that he now believed he had been wrong in dismissing so easily the possibility of this kind of long-distance control. Then he apologised for the incoherence of his expression. It was not very easy, he said, to write coherently when every sentence you wrote was immediately repeated by a bodiless voice.

This is all I remember of his letters, and I think it was all that at that time he said. But it was enough. Not merely the matter but the manner of these letters was so totally unlike Evelyn – the sadly apologetic air, the defeated spirit . . . Only the handwriting convinced one they were written by him.

Laura said she felt someone must go and fetch him back. She had thought it over and believed it must be a man, partly in case Evelyn was getting into trouble, but chiefly because – in spite of the dispirited letters – he might be belligerently unwilling to accept this kind of interference. She asked Jack if he would go.

It was immediately arranged that she should give him a cheque for a sufficient sum of money and that he would take the first aeroplane. But when he came to make the arrangements he found that he could not enter Colombo without a certificate of inoculation against typhoid – a paper which takes ten days to obtain. We considered whether he should nevertheless go and either bribe or force his way in, a thing Laura said Evelyn had often done in the past in other countries. Finally it was decided that both he and Laura should have the first of the injections and go together before the second only if it seemed absolutely necessary. Before the period was up Evelyn solved the difficulty by announcing by cable that he was on his way home.

When Laura asked Jack to go she warned us that she thought it possible that, when Evelyn recovered his mind, he might be so angry that she had confided in us that it would spoil our friendship forever. Consequently, when she went to London to meet him we did not expect to hear, unless privately from her, any news of either of them for several weeks. When she discussed with me what she was going to say and do when she met him, I felt very much frightened, because she proposed to behave as one would to a person who is sane, whereas it seemed to me that

Evelyn was quite clearly insane. I thought her approach should be more tentative and more subtle. However, she was immovable in her opinion.

Two, or possibly three, days later, to our intense surprise we received a message saying that the Waughs were on their way back to Piers Court and Evelyn wished us to go to dinner.

When we walked into the room there he was, looking extremely thin, which suited him, but otherwise apparently perfectly normal and in the highest good spirits. He greeted Jack with some words showing that he knew of the typhoid inoculation.

'A thing,' he said, 'I would do for no man.'

Then between them they told us this story.

As Laura walked up the stairs of the Hyde Park Hotel she heard a voice ask in a high, unrecognizable squeak whether she had yet arrived. She looked up and to her surprise saw Evelyn. She said that his voice was distorted by disuse, because for weeks he had spoken to no one. I have no idea whether this is a likely effect.

As soon as they reached their bedroom Evelyn began to tell Laura what had happened to him. He said that on board ship there had been a family named Black. The father of this family was someone they knew. He was the man who had interrogated him in a broadcast interview he had recently given. This man had a wife, a son and a daughter and the whole family used the infernal powers he had told her about to persecute him. Only the daughter showed any mercy, and she at times seemed to pity him. This girl he told Laura they also knew. She was engaged to a young man – he mentioned the name – who lived in Wotton-under-Edge and who had brought her to luncheon at Piers Court.

'But Evelyn,' Laura objected, 'that girl's name wasn't Black, it was So-and-So, and she had nothing to do with the BBC man.'

Laura said that when she said this Evelyn saw almost at once it was true. He reacted to this startling piece of information in the manner of the sane. They discussed the details for some time and Laura tried to persuade him that he had been ill and must see a doctor. Very well, he replied, but before doing so they would test other links in his story. He took command of the situation, devised a plan and told Laura how to carry it out. On his instructions she telephoned to the BBC and asked to speak to Mr Black. To her horror the answering voice said that Mr Black was at present away. She asked where he was and when he was expected to return, and then she was told that he had been in hospital for some weeks and, although he was recovering from his illness, it was not yet known when he would return.

So much for Mr and Miss Black. Yet Evelyn could still hear their voices. They decided at this point to ask Father Caraman to come round to advise them and, when he arrived, they told him the whole of this story. Father Caraman sent at once for the late E. B. Strauss, a psycho-analyst who was also a Roman Catholic. Strauss said, and later other doctors confirmed this view, that Evelyn was suffering from the quantities of chloral he had absorbed in the weeks before he went away. He said that if he had eaten and slept properly he would have quickly recovered. But in all these weeks Evelyn had been unable either to eat or sleep. Strauss proceeded to ensure him a night's rest by administering a different drug – paraldehyde – and he persuaded him to eat. Now here he was still, he said, occasionally and faintly hearing the voices but otherwise entirely recovered.

Up to this point the story had been told, with interruptions, by Laura. Now Evelyn took it over.

His behaviour seemed to us extraordinary and as usual completely unexpected. Laura, who in my opinion is the only person who has ever had the slightest idea of how Evelyn really thought and felt, had believed that he might be irreconcilably put against us by the knowledge that we had been told of his misfortunes. But on the contrary he seemed not merely in the highest good humour, but apparently extremely pleased with himself. He had the air of someone who has brought off an unexpected coup or discovered in himself some unsuspected gift, I, who have what I believe to be a normal horror of madness, was much relieved that chloral and not inherent weakness had caused the mental aberration through which he had passed. But Evelyn, then and ever after, chose to behave as though he had had a true mental breakdown. Either immediately before we saw him or soon afterwards he met a woman friend in London who said:

'Oh, Evelyn, I hear you've been ill. I hope you are better.'

Evelyn burst into laughter and replied: 'I know that

Laura has been putting it about that I've been ill. But it isn't true. I've been off my head.'

I think he was immensely attracted by madness. This is a passage from *The Loved One.*

> Her hair was dark and straight, her brows wide, her skin transparent and untarnished by sun. Her lips were artificially tinctured, no doubt, but not coated like her sisters' and clogged in their delicate pores with crimson grease; they seemed to promise instead an unmeasured range of sensual converse. Her full face was oval, her profile pure and classical and light. Her eyes greenish and remote, with a rich glint of lunacy.
>
> Dennis held his breath.

Evelyn was always tremendously diverted by the spectacle of someone making an ass of himself. On this evening his illness was so close to him that it was still slightly upon him, and, if proof were needed for the genuineness of his suffering, we had it in his letters and on his thin face. Yet he told the story with a detachment and a mockery that if he had been speaking of some other person would have seemed, as he often did seem, inhumanly cruel and insensitive. It was not merely that the element of self-pity was entirely missing; although he had recovered his senses only two or three days before, he quite clearly regarded his misadventures as outrageously funny. In him the sense of the ridiculous was much stronger than the kinder emotions. Somewhere, in words I can neither remember nor find, he has described how, when he first entered Forest Lawn, the

Evelyn outside Combe Florey

Evelyn in the sitting-room at Combe Florey

Hollywood cemetery featured in *The Loved One*, an instinct stirring within him told him that something awaited him here. This first night at home I think he was happy to be there, to be free of his persecutors, but his exaltation may have been due to his yet unconscious knowledge that he was in possession of a new creation. We could not be aware of this, however, and we listened simply astounded.

He began as he had in his letters and as I think he also did in *Pinfold* by saying that he had at first believed that there were some people in the next cabin who were deliberately trying to annoy him. He could not completely hear their conversation but he could hear that his name again and again recurred. During the night this continued and he was unable to sleep. He had resolved to ignore this – very unlike him – until he recognized some words of his own and he realized that copies of some cables he had sent to England were being read out loud. Then he went to the Captain.

He told the Captain that in the cabin next to his there was a family who interfered with his peace. He would not have complained about this but he felt that one ought to be able to put complete trust in the discretion of the radio operator. He was sorry to have to say it, but copies of cables he had sent to England had been passed to this family.

The Captain replied to this with complete gravity and courtesy. He said there was only one family on board ship and they were not in a cabin anywhere near Evelyn's. He suggested that they go together to interview the radio operator. This they did and the Captain asked the operator for copies of the cables Evelyn had sent to England. The operator replied that he had sent only one, on the first day out. He produced a copy of this cable which was addressed to Laura and merely said that he was well.

Evelyn believed the Captain and the operator, but, as he had to account for the voices which grew louder and more persistent, he then evolved the theory of long-range telepathy. He also went to the bar in an effort to meet the one mysterious family. Here he met 'Mr Black' whom he recognized immediately as an enemy, his wife, his son and his daughter, whom only later when she began to take pity on him did he recognize as the girl who had come to luncheon. While he was with them they talked normally in their own voices and telepathically in their persecuting voices, and he realized he was up against a fiendish combination.

This conversation took place more than ten years ago and I cannot remember it in detail. There were, however, three set pieces.

In the first Evelyn had become convinced from words overheard that a serious attempt to harm him was to be made at night in his cabin. Dressed in his pyjamas and a coat with a stick in his hand – I think with a bowler hat on his head but Jack cannot remember this – he waited throughout the night outside his cabin door, lonely, and brave, to repel the expected attack. Nothing happened.

In the second, unable to sleep, he wandered alone on the deck again at night. He became aware that in the silence a group of people were taking part in some great activity.

Lurking, preposterous in his pyjamas, in the background, he watched a ship draw alongside and he saw the Captain of his own ship in command of a small party of men transfer to the other ship a stretcher which held a dead body. The following morning he congratulated the Captain on the efficiency of the operation.

The third concerned his partial triumph over the voices. He believed by the time he flew home and before he met Laura that he was already beginning to recover, and with the first strength he could command he began the counter-attack. The weapon he chose and the success which attended his efforts provided the most grotesque incident of all. In or near Stinchcombe there lived at that time a beautiful and charming old maiden lady. On Sunday mornings, after she had attended matins in the Anglican church and the Waughs mass in the Roman Catholic one she used often to call at Piers Court for a glass of sherry. Evelyn now discovered that the family Black were in some way related to this old lady and he threatened them with exposure of their persecution to her. Soon he had them cowering in fear and begging him not to proceed to this horrible reprisal. Evelyn acted these scenes of their fear and his dominating use of this powerful name, and the humour of the situation lay in the fact that, in the sense that they had appeared to him, these things were true. Evelyn, the merciless, thrice-armed, self-reliant terror of the sane world had, in his insanity, adopted for his shield this gentle, ineffectual old lady.

I asked him whether the Captain of the ship had seemed

glad to be rid of him, and he replied that, if so, he had been unaware of it. He had been treated with kindness and courtesy. Only one incident had struck him as odd. While in Ceylon he had run into a young man who had been on the ship. This young man had looked at him sorrowfully and asked him if he was feeling better. Evelyn who was not aware of having been ill could not understand his concern.

Since writing the preceding words I have re-read *Pinfold*. It is tempting to correct the mistakes of memory, but there is the consideration that, to anyone who has knowledge of such things, a memory completely accurate over a period of twelve years is even more suspect than one that is normally fallible.

So first of all, here is a small point: the MA was the Medical Attendant not the Medical Adviser. Secondly, I incline to think there was no bowler hat. But, far more difficult to explain away, Evelyn in *Pinfold* gives not merely an accurate but a lovingly lavish description of the intake of bromide and chloral. Having explained to the chemist that it is a waste of bottle space for him to dilute the mixture with water when this can so easily be done at home, Mr Pinfold mixes it neat with *crème de menthe* and sloshes it down whenever the inclination takes him; whereas I had believed that he went off his head without the aid of any outside agency. However, I seem not to be alone in this mistake. Evelyn's son says in the article already quoted: 'When my father was eventually driven mad by the jackals snarling and whining around his ankles . . . All the malicious sneers . . . directed at him in his lifetime came home to roost until, by an iron effort of the will, he sent them back to Fleet Street and the obituary columns.'

But Evelyn made no iron effort of will – although by nature he was entirely capable of it – he simply ceased to overdose himself with chloral and recovered when the effects of it had left his body. I think the misapprehension is due to two things. The first is that, although he wrote accurately of what had happened, conversationally he always preferred to treat his experience as a short period of madness. Secondly, it may be that most people are not aware of the effect of strong doses of chloral. Evelyn himself knew all about it because in his youth he wrote a life of Rossetti.

In all other respects my memory is pedestrianly accurate. All the actual happenings and the incidents he described in detail are here in the book as close to reality as suits the conventions of a novel, although it may interest those who regard him as lacking in courtesy to his fellows to note that, in the case of the ally with whose aid he finally beat off the voices, he changed both the name and the sex.

However, I am reminded of one rather amusing thing. In *Pinfold* Evelyn describes a present given to Mr Pinfold by a friend: 'a wash-hand stand of the greatest elaboration designed by an English architect of the 1850s, a man not universally honoured but of magisterial status to Mr Pinfold and his friends', with panels 'painted in his hot youth by a rather preposterous artist who later became President of the Royal Academy'. When this wash-hand stand is delivered to his home (this is before he undertakes his journey) Mr Pinfold is extremely upset because a highly ornamental copper tap forming the climax of the design is missing. He makes the carriers search the van, signs the receipt 'incomplete' and writes a complaint to the firm enclosing a drawing of the lost tap. Finally he writes to the friend who gave him the present asking for his corroboration that the tap should be there, only to be told that it had never existed. On looking back on his experiences this seems to Mr Pinfold the first sign of his mental disturbance.

All these things happened to Evelyn. The wash-hand stand designed by William Burges with panels painted by Sir Edward Poynton was given him by John Betjeman and when it was delivered he did go through all these motions of trying to recover a tap which existed only in his imagination. However, at the time, although we were very much amused by the story of his aberration, it did not occur to us – at any rate not to Jack and me – that it was sufficiently abnormal to suggest mental disturbance. It often happens that people remember things wrongly, even things they have liked very much and examined very closely. It is more usual to forget details than to invent them but we were accustomed to the ceaseless working of Evelyn's imagination. For instance, on one occasion, years before this time, he had been very anxious that we should all go together to see the film of *Monsieur Verdoux* in Dursley because he had enjoyed it so much in London. As we came out of the cinema at the end of the film, Laura,

Jack and I spoke of it with pleasure, saying how amusing we had found it. Evelyn was deeply disappointed. He said that so many of the funniest scenes he remembered had, on this occasion, not been there.

Nevertheless, on the second reading I still find *Pinfold* a disappointing book. It starts admittedly with some of the most brilliant pages he ever wrote – astonishing both for the extent of the revelations and the quality of the writing – but from the moment Mr Pinfold arrives on the boat I find his story, though similar in detail, infinitely less moving than the one that Evelyn told to us. The figure that he described on his return home, baffled and lonely but bravely battling against unknown and uncontrollable forces, had a true affinity with all the best tragi-comic creations in history – Charlie Chaplin at once springs to mind. Then too the Captain in this story was throughout a grave and courteous person, accepting politely Evelyn's revelations about his radio operator and his mysterious congratulations on the efficiency of some unaccomplished naval operation, while the daughter of the persecuting family was an innocent maiden moved by pity for the sufferings of a stranger. In *Pinfold* the Captain is at one moment a torturer with a female accomplice whose counterpart can be found in most thrillers from Sapper's *Bulldog Drummond* to Ian Fleming's *From Russia With Love*, while the daughter's interest in Pinfold is of a sexual and, to me, embarrassing kind.

It is clearly possible that the second is the 'true' story and that there were details of his experience which Evelyn did not care to describe to us. Equally there are indications in the book that the novelist is practising his art which support my view that the real happenings differed from those related there. Here is an example. Evelyn invariably and rather maliciously referred to people whose English name might have been derived from some German or Jewish equivalent by what he conceived to have been the original. Anyone whose name ended in 'don' or 'ston' or 'den' always received a rich and lingering 'stein', while Waterman, for instance, might become Wasserman. In one of the scenes of the persecution of Mr Pinfold the bullying voices insist that his real name is Peinfeld and that he is a German and a Jew. It is difficult to see how this can be anything but a later invention when one remembers that the real sufferer from these unreal assailants had a good Scottish name impossible to distort in this way.

Probably his experiences were too blurred and too diffuse to do more than inspire *The Ordeal of Gilbert Pinfold* and Evelyn naturally used his gifts to improve the theme he had so painfully acquired. It would not have disturbed him in the least to know that I thought he had failed.

Chapter 5

INCOME TAX

EVELYN was a great devotee of P.G. Wodehouse. Jack and I had both for many years known the Master – I since I was a child and Jack since a young man, and it was in the house of his step-daughter we first met. We proudly claimed this friendship and educated Evelyn to the fact that to his friends Wodehouse is known as Plummy. Evelyn had a nearly complete edition of his works which was specially bound in leather. The books published up to the time of his marriage had been given to him and he had later bound many – I think not all – of the books which subsequently appeared to match the others. However, Jack owned a rarity, an early book named *Swoop* of which Evelyn had not heard, and which had been given him by Wodehouse himself. This book was in a paperback edition and becoming slightly spoilt. Jack was glad both to be able to give Evelyn an unusual present and to find a leather binding which would preserve the Master's present to him. He gave it to Evelyn in 1948, the first Christmas after we met him.

Later he gave him two books he had picked up on a bookstall as a young man and which were by this time rarities. This present elicited the following letter.

My dear Jack,

What a delicious Christmas present. The *William Tell told Again* is a bibliographical gem of purest quality. I have never seen a copy before or heard of it except from you. It is the rarest thing to find a children's book in library condition.

And the Master as critic in a *Century of Humour* is most interesting and a necessary part of a Wodehouse collection which I lacked.

Thank you so much for giving it to me. I do hope that Thomas will not later reproach you with the dispersal of heirlooms.

I hope your Christmas was cloudless. Ours was ghastly but it is over. I would prefer a week of Ash Wednesdays, but I discovered a senile taste for mince pies.

I hope we see you both again soon.

Yours ever
Evelyn

Although I had known Plummy Wodehouse most of my life and his daughter – who died before this time – had been one of my greatest friends, I had never been able to read his books. I cannot see the point of them. For years I allowed myself to believe that he is a man's writer, that it is normal as a woman not to enjoy him. But as my own children grew up, two of them daughters, I found that they and most of their friends read all the old volumes of Wodehouse and bought, either for themselves or as presents for their father, the new books as they came out. He is, it seems, one of the very few writers who is never out of date, a joy to each succeeding generation. But even acknowledging this I still, like Wodehouse himself I believe, have never been able to understand the 'Master' stuff. I therefore questioned Evelyn about this.

'One has to regard a man as a Master,' he replied, 'who can produce on average three uniquely brilliant and entirely original similies to every page.'

It therefore greatly amused him to learn from the autobiographical books and also from letters he himself received later from Plummy, that the part of his work on which Wodehouse prided himself most and which to him was the only source of difficulty or anxiety was the working out of the plots.

During the Wodehouse troubles of the war years Evelyn had, unasked, rushed in writing to his defence. About the time of which I speak many English writers contributed short appreciative pieces for some memorial to Wodehouse, I think on his seventieth birthday, and Evelyn again wrote something. He received a letter of thanks.

That night we dined at Piers Court and Evelyn showed us the letter. He said he had been in a great difficulty to know how to reply. The letter he received had begun 'Dear Evelyn . . .' Evelyn could not reply 'Dear Wodehouse . . .' for fear of seeming cold, nor 'Dear P. G. Wodehouse . . .' because he detested this form of address, nor 'Dear Plummy . . .' in the simple manner that Plummy had addressed him, because he did not know him.

'I think, however,' he said with pride, 'that I have found the solution. I have put "Dear Dr Wodehouse".'

Ever after this he referred to him and addressed him in this manner.

Once, however, he met him. There has grown up a belief or it might be truer to say that a belief was put about by Evelyn himself that he hated America and almost all Americans. This may for reasons I do not know have become true. When we first knew him he was making a great deal of money there, he had at least a few close personal friends who lived there, and for two or three years he visited New York each autumn. On one of these occasions a public luncheon was given for him by the editress of *Vogue*, who asked him whether there was any particular person he would like to have invited. He immediately named P. G. Wodehouse. His hostess replied that if he wished Mr Wodehouse to be asked he must invite him himself, and Evelyn went to some pains to do this. When he returned he told us that Plummy had come to the luncheon and been given the place of honour next to him.

'Well . . .' we asked.

Evelyn gave his expostulatory chuckle.

'It was not very amusing,' he said, 'I could not persuade him to talk on any subject except income tax.'

Evelyn himself was never a bore about income tax. He did not regard it as a topic for conversation. But his resentment at paying over so large a part of his earnings to the State affected adversely the latter part of his life and restricted his output as a writer. A burning sense of injustice cannot be avoided in a situation where any small industrialist can still find ways to build up his capital, while the writer, whose talent is usually a fluctuating or diminishing asset, can never guard against old age or loss of power or popularity, because his income – with certain concessions – is treated like that of a salary earner while he has none of the security this nowadays implies.

Evelyn believed that an imaginative writer has only a limited store on which to draw. This is not an uncommon idea. Max Beerbohm said:

> Nine lustres exhaust from a writer any vital stuff that may be in him. The question is not of the amount he has to express, but simply of the time during which he has tried to express it. The small writer aged 30 will have relatively as much left in him as the great writer aged 30; and neither will have anything to express fifteen years later.

I think Evelyn saw the matter less as one of time and more as one of quantity. He believed that each writer has only two or three themes and that when he has worked these out he has nothing 'vital' left in him. He was always immensely grateful when, as in the case of *The Loved One* or *The Ordeal of Gilbert Pinfold* he was presented with an idea from outside the mainstream of his experience and invention. He said of the latter book: 'It is a great piece of luck for a middle-aged writer to be presented with an entirely new theme.' He used to speak critically of a lack of technique in other people – 'He has used the material for six books in one' – and he referred again and again to the possibility that his own creative powers might one day be exhausted, remarking that he supposed he could always earn a living writing biography and book reviews.

Once when I was talking to him about my father I said I thought men with a small or particular talent were able to push this to its extreme when they were young because of their freedom from responsibility to any personal standard. In middle age they seemed to become too scrupulous, too concerned with the import of their work.

'It is no longer enough, for instance, simply to be funny.'

'Perhaps,' he replied lugubriously, 'they no longer feel funny.'

Here is a letter he wrote me to prove that it is impossible for a writer to earn more than a limited annual income even allowing for certain concessions the tax laws make him.

Piers Court
Stinchcombe
8 May 54

Dear Frankie,

Lady Browning's income: 100,000 copies @ 12/6 produce a 20% royalty of £12,500 i.e. difference between sale of 100,000 and 150,000=gross £6,250.

Suppose her previous thrift to qualify her for full Welfare rates of taxation:

Gross £6,250=net (approx.) £156.

Yours ever
Evelyn

Lady Browning is known to the public as Daphne du Maurier and I had chosen her in conversation as one of the few writers who hits the jackpot with every book. A writer of Evelyn's quality cannot expect to do this more than once or twice in a lifetime. It seems not to be generally known that the early books that made his name and were written before the days of heavy taxation achieved fame but only limited sales at the time of publication.

The meaning of his letter may not be entirely clear, nor the facts completely accurate. But the point is that while on all his earnings the writer pays tax and supertax, he can neither by hard work nor unusual success raise these earnings in good years to save against bad. Evelyn had six children to educate.

When we first knew him he had a beautiful house and an adequate staff of servants, but his standard of living seemed not immoderate to us. I think at that time his accountants were engaged in one of those long wrangles over back tax which so often produce devastating effects when a settlement is reached. In any case, although he ranked among writers as one of England's largest earners he was never free from worry about money or about the insecurity of his future. Quite early in our friendship the staff of servants left Piers Court to be replaced by an Italian couple, and in the later years of his life at Combe Florey there were no household servants, and Laura managed everything with the help of dailies.

When he died he left a house which is said to be of considerable value (although if this is so it is because the value of property in England has quadrupled since he bought it), his library and his collection of pictures and furniture. His liquid assets, according to his published will, amounted to £11,000. These facts explain, if they are not thought to justify, some preoccupation with the subject of money and an aversion to the social philosophy which hit him so much harder than it hit the local builder.

I have always believed, perhaps fancifully, that income tax spoiled the end of his life. I have said enough here to show that he was by nature largely recluse, fitfully gregarious. He used to enjoy entertaining at Piers Court, his occasional visits to London and above all his annual travels. When he could no longer do these things in style he became more and more recluse and misanthropic, more and more melancholy.

Whether or not I am right in my view, the happy days at Piers Court came to an end in 1956. Evelyn began to be restless, ostensibly because he believed the town of Dursley was creeping up to his gates, but really I think because he wished for change, to break the rut of boredom in which he was sunk. Certainly Laura consented to leave the house she loved because she hoped the change might be good for him.

At Combe Florey he seemed more than ever cut off from his friends, he went less and less to London, fewer and fewer people stayed with him. One began to get the impression that he simply awaited death. In any case, as far as I am concerned, the halcyon days were at Piers Court. Here he was still young and gay, here he wrote his best books, *The Loved One*, *Helena*, and the first volume of the trilogy.

Sadly we parted, with many promises of visits to be interchanged; but although they remained among our dearest friends, we never saw very much of them again.

Evelyn in the grounds of Combe Florey

Evelyn writing

Evelyn at work in his new library

PART TWO

COMBE FLOREY

Chapter 6

VISITS TO SOMERSET

WHEN the Waughs left Gloucestershire in 1956 we consoled ourselves with the idea that we would stay with them very often and Laura, if not Evelyn, with us. We were, I think, their first guests and among the last before Evelyn died in 1966, and, in the years between, we stayed there at fairly regular intervals. There were two reasons why we went much less often than we had thought we would. The first was the ordinary one that Combe Florey was far away and difficult to get to, and, when we ourselves moved from Gloucestershire to Buckinghamshire, we doubled the distance between us. From our long knowledge of the household we did not believe it sensible to stay longer than one night or at the very most two, and it was difficult to find time to motor so far very often.

There was, however, a second reason, and in the interests of accuracy and possibly of credibility I must try to explain it. Even before the Waughs left Gloucestershire there had been a slight loss of warmth between Evelyn and me. At this time I was writing a book about my father, who was by now dead. One evening we were discussing, not the book but an incident in his life about which I was writing, when Evelyn suddenly was angrily and grossly insulting about him. I could not forgive him and I loved him less; Evelyn, so perceptive in these things, loved me less in return. This is how I saw it; it may not be what happened. It may be that Evelyn was bored with me, or irritated by something I was not aware of, and the whole thing started one remove further back.

I think that, if there had been only Evelyn and me, our friendship might have ceased at that time, but there were Laura and Jack, and, on a new level, we went on much as before. Certainly I felt very sad when they left, and for several years visited them regularly.

Then there came a period when during our visits to Combe Florey it seemed apparent that Evelyn was either angry with me or again perhaps merely bored. He was occasionally mildly offensive and his manner to me was noticeably lacking in warmth. No one who knew him would regard it as unnecessarily touchy to be frightened of him in this mood. But what made me feel certain of a coldness between us was that twice, when sending us a copy of a new book, he inscribed it to Jack and not me. I was not merely hurt and disappointed, I was also angry, because I saw this as an intentional snub. The first book was the life of Ronald Knox and the second a little book he wrote for a shipping company in return for a trip to Africa. Jack and Jack McDougall (the chairman of Chapman & Hall and his publisher) both tried to persuade me that in the first case, since I was known not to be a believer in the Christian faith, I might be thought not to be interested in Knox; and, in the second, the book was one he did not care for himself, but sent to Jack in return for an introduction to someone who had been useful to him in Africa. I remained unconvinced, because, although these might be adequate excuses, I thought Evelyn in a friendly mood would not have had need of them.

He approved of the adage 'never apologize, never explain'. No one, I think, would ever have said to him, as one might to almost anyone else I have ever known: what is it that has gone wrong between us? There was the hideous risk he might tell you. If Evelyn's moods were irrational, his justification for them was apt to be lacerating. I simply refused to go to Combe Florey.

Now that he is dead and I have gone through his letters, I can see that if this loss of favour occurred – and one can never be sure of anything because Evelyn inspired over-sensitivity in other people – it was of fairly short duration, because I have affectionate letters from him written at an interval of about eighteen months, during which interval the two books were published. Soon after I was persuaded to risk one more visit to Combe Florey on Laura's account, and on this occasion all was sweetness and light and Evelyn as friendly as before. He was also so amusing that I – the only time that I did so – wrote down all I could remember of his conversation immediately on our return home. The last chapter of this book is the record of that time. But by now he was becoming old and ill and we never again went very often.

I am so glad we ended in amity and glad too that I know no more of what passed between us than I have recorded.

He maintained unbroken affection for Jack because Jack is so difficult to offend. He is very amiable, very confident and unshakeably tolerant of small teases. Evelyn, for instance, always addressed him on postcards and envelopes as Colonel Donaldson, although he knew he had dropped his wartime rank, in order to be able to put after his name the letters RAOC or RASC, although he also knew he had served in the Royal Engineers. Those aware of the relative status of the different army corps will appreciate the subtleties of this joke, which Jack also thought rather funny. However, on one of our last visits to Combe Florey a small thing occurred which, before leaving the subject of our relations with Evelyn, I must record.

Staying at Combe Florey, Jack and I went one afternoon for a walk and Jack, wanting a stick, rather stupidly chose a light cane. This he broke, and on our return went shamefacedly to Evelyn to apologize. Evelyn was really upset and angry – he loved this small, rather dashing cane – and Jack felt an ass. When we got home he wrote to Evelyn asking him to send it to Briggs to be mended but Evelyn replied: 'Tonkin has been spliced locally', and Jack forgot the incident.

Some weeks later I said to him, not thinking much about it:

'Annie had a letter from Evelyn in which he said: "The Donaldsons came to stay. He broke my cane.".'

'Oh no,' Jack cried. 'How beastly of him.'

The short, deflating sentences, the lugubrious disloyalty touched Jack where years of highly skilled teases had failed.

He knew that, although we had travelled a long way, although on the whole everyone had enjoyed the visit, the only thing Evelyn remembered about it was that Jack broke his cane.

Chapter 7

LETTERS AND POSTCARDS

FROM Combe Florey we naturally received many more letters from Evelyn than when he lived near us at Piers Court. I have picked out a few for inclusion here, some because they seem amusing as they stand, some because they remind me of some characteristic incident.

It is not possible to give them in chronological order because Evelyn seldom dated his letters. This is so surprising in someone so meticulous by nature that when – on re-reading his letters after his death – I first noticed it I thought there must be some absurd reason for it – such as that earlier it had been the custom of the trade to date letters but not of the gentry. This seems, however, not to be so and it remains an unaccountable fact that will prove a great nuisance to the future editor of his letters. A few letters we have from him are dated, and there is a suggestion of a possible method because these are nearly all to thank for a present or to confirm some engagement. Often it is possible to date his communications because he was addicted to postcards, which carry a postmark.

For years it was Evelyn's practice to examine everything written about him in the newspapers in an attempt to detect grounds for a libel action. His interest in the matter was exactly comparable to other people's interest in football pools or the Irish Sweepstake. He regarded it as the only hope of acquiring a large sum of money not subject to tax. When Randolph Churchill successfully challenged a newspaper which had described him as a 'hack', Evelyn, filled with admiration and glee, was spurred on to the chase.

His opportunity came following a call made upon him by Nancy Spain of the *Daily Express*, accompanied, for some reason no one ever understood, by Lord Noel Buxton. This call received great publicity at the time, but has probably been forgotten now. What happened roughly was this. Miss Spain telephoned to Piers Court to ask if she might come to interview Evelyn and was told by Laura that he was working and unable to see anyone. Undaunted she presently arrived at the front door of the house in company with her escort, and Laura, again barring the passage to Evelyn, could not, nevertheless, induce her to leave. Presently, disturbed by the noise, Evelyn himself appeared and, with words which if I ever knew them I have forgotten, succeeded where Laura had failed.

The matter might have ended here, but Miss Spain, not to be done out of material for her column, recorded what had passed for the *Daily Express*. Then at some point in the publicity which followed the incident, she made an unguarded statement comparing the sales of Evelyn's books inaccurately and unfavourably with the sales of his brother Alec's.

At last! Evelyn sent the paragraph off to his lawyer and

received the assurance that an action would have a reasonable chance of success.

When the great day came Mr Gerald Gardiner appeared for Evelyn, Sir Hartley Shawcross for the *Daily Express*. The latter was called away in the middle of the case because of the illness of his mother, but not before he had cross-examined Evelyn. Evelyn gave evidence soberly and quietly – no fireworks – and admitted afterwards to a feeling of uneasiness when confronted by Shawcross. Laura, bravely, and Alec Waugh, loyally, gave evidence on his behalf. The afternoon of the first day passed with Miss Spain in the witness box denying hour after hour the undeniable. This bland effort which consisted of taking a different view of the meaning of everything, including words, from that taken by anyone else, may or may not have been prejudicial to the outcome of the case. In spite of it the judge summing up the next morning reduced the Waugh party to the depths of gloom by luncheon, since it seemed likely that Evelyn would get a farthing's damages. This would have been a serious outcome because he would have been left with costs of about £1,000. However, the jury returned to the court in the afternoon and awarded him £5,000.

At this time the Waughs were moving into Combe Florey and a very beautiful rug copied by the Wilton factory from a Victorian original decorates the drawing-room floor to commemorate the case.

Soon after this Jack received a letter from Evelyn enclosing a cutting from the Dursley *Gazette* which reported Jack's speech at a local meeting and described him as a 'mucky boots farmer', a term which is used to mean a farmer who works on the farm himself. The following paragraph occurred in the article:

> Mr Donaldson is a large-scale wheat and barley grower on a farm bought by his wife while he was in the Army, and keeps up to 100 cows and 200 ewes.

The letter accompanying this reads as follows:

> I send this in case you have not seen it. It is certainly actionable suggesting that you are physically unclean and the enemy of the gentry. Moreover I think a clever lawyer could argue that 'mucky' suggested sexual impurity. 'Mucking' was much used for 'fucking' in novels of the 50s. May I recommend my man Rubinstein of Rubinstein Nash. There is also a plain lie in saying your estate was bought behind your marital back by Frankie. Can you prove personal malice on the part of Winter? If so, you are in a good position.

This was written on a postcard from Combe Florey but the cutting was from a Gloucestershire paper, which suggests that it was the first time Evelyn wrote to us from his new home.

On the Sunday after Evelyn's death Michael Frayn told a story about him in the column he writes for the *Observer*. He said that a friend of his had gone to the wedding party of one of Evelyn's daughters in an everyday suit, and, finding that everyone else was dressed in morning coat, had apologized to Evelyn. Evelyn had replied: 'I should sack your man.'

This was very rum indeed. Soon after the Waughs went to Combe Florey Alice Jolliffe (Sweet Alice), now grown up, came to stay with us in Gloucestershire and told us a story she had lately been told by Evelyn. She said that Alan Pryce Jones went once in his youth to stay with Lord Clinton, packing in his bag a dinner-jacket. When he went down to dinner he found everyone else in tails, and he apologized to his host saying that he had not brought a tail-suit.

Lord Clinton replied kindly: 'I should sack your man.'

Jack proceeded to correct Alice. He had been told this story as a young man by Edward Marsh and it had always been one of his favourites. I had heard him tell it a dozen times. However, he did not think it was about Alan Pryce Jones or Lord Clinton but about Eddie Marsh himself and someone else. He told Alice he thought that since Evelyn knew the story, he must have learned it from him, but he had got the facts wrong. This conversation took place at some meal in our house and was quickly forgotten by us. A few weeks later he received the following on a postcard from Evelyn:

Postmark 4.8.57

The story of Jones and Lord Clinton ('sack your man') was told to me by Eddie Marsh shortly after the event, about 20 years ago. It culminated in the far more humiliating incident of the coffee cup at breakfast next day which drove Jones from the house. *You never told me*

> *either story*. It is possible that in his dotage Eddie related the experience as his own. You should not impugn my credibility to the young. I think you are bound in honour to explain your mistake to Miss Jolliffe.

Jack wrote in reply that he was sorry he had made a mistake. He thought, nevertheless, that Evelyn should not be so quick to anger with his old friends. He made no mention of the suggestion in the last sentence of Evelyn's postcard. This produced the following on a postcard with a postmark two days later than the first:

> Postmark 6.8.57
> Mr E.W. C.F.
>
> I am distressed that you should think my zeal for the truth unmannerly. Had Eddie's story been Edwardian, it would not have been worth telling for tail-coats were always worn at house-parties in that reign. In the 30s Lord Clinton was a very eccentric survival. Perhaps Eddie did not tell you the subsequent breakfast incident. I will do so when we meet – which I hope may be soon.

Satisfactory, we thought – the nearest to an apology anyone was likely to receive. The story of the breakfast incident had already been told us by Evelyn, who had been told it originally by Eddie Marsh, not by Alan Pryce Jones, who, oddly, never appears in this except as the original narrator of these stories to Marsh.

On the morning following 'Sack your man', Alan Pryce Jones, arriving down to breakfast before his host, helped himself to coffee and sat down at the table. Presently Lord Clinton appeared.

'Is that coffee you're drinking?' he asked.

His guest replied that it was.

'But you've got a tea cup.' Then reproachfully: '*Not* very nice for the next person who wants to drink tea.'

Because Harold Hobson praised *Waiting for Godot* he was given a copy of the Paris edition of *Lolita* by the French publisher who was also Samuel Beckett's publisher. Arriving to stay with us for Christmas he gave this to Jack, who thus acquired one of the very few copies to reach England at that time. He lent this to various people including Evelyn. Later from Combe Florey he received a post-card from Evelyn:

> Postmark 18 Nov. 1958
>
> Laura says she 'half invited' you & Frankie for Monday night next, Nov 24th. May I wholly invite you?
>
> *Lolita*. I only remember the smut. The Yankee edition is full of very high-brow allusions. It set me wondering whether there was a modern counterpart of Bowdler (who excised smut from works of literary merit) whose office is to introduce 'literary merit' into smut. If in your corrupt Court circles you know anyone who has a copy of the Paris edition, do get it for me. It may be a mare's nest but if I have hit on the truth it will be jolly funny.

It was a mare's nest.

Jack had all his life had a number of moles on his face. In his early fifties he began to grow lumps on his forehead of the kind often to be seen on the faces of old gentlemen which are caused by some kind of calcification. He decided to have these removed, partly because they were very ugly, partly because we all have a superstitious feeling about lumps. He went to a surgeon in Bristol who advised him to allow him also to remove a few of the moles. On receiving Jack's permission to do this he quickly removed the whole lot, thereby significantly altering Jack's appearance. At the same time June Osborn went to a different man in London to have some moles removed and this man turned out to be a friend of Jack's, a colleague who had played with him in the Cambridge jazz band in the halcyon days of Fred Elizalde. Meat and drink to Evelyn. He began with a postcard from Combe Florey.

Postmark 14.4.61.

Alas, no sherry here now. We hope to bottle some soon. I am told you have had your face reconditioned by June Capel's plastic surgeon. True?

E.

Soon after this wherever we went someone looked carefully at Jack.

'Let me see your face. Evelyn tells me . . .'

A second post-card arrived.

Postmark 24.4.1961.

I should like to see your beautiful new face. Can you bring it to luncheon at White's on Friday.

Four months later Jack's face was still of interest to Evelyn.

Postmark 3.8.61.

Thanks awfully for your post-card. My daughter, Margaret, saw you in London and was much struck by your beauty since your operation. I have not had recourse to June's jazz drummer but I was so shocked by a photograph of me that appeared after Bron's wedding that I have fasted ever since and am now beautiful too. I see in the morning paper that fasting is now punishable by law in India. I hope you like Bill Deakin – an admirable young hero.

E.

This series of post-cards and the interest in Jack's face shown by so many of Evelyn's friends suggest that, like other wits before him, notably Oscar Wilde, he sometimes worked his jokes hard, sending them to each of his correspondents at the same time. He mentioned Bill Deakin because my daughter Rose had become engaged to his son. The Warden of St Antony's College, Oxford, F. W. Deakin had earned Evelyn's admiration for his unpublicised gallantry while working with the resistance movement in Yugoslavia during the war.

The following letter is a particularly good example of Evelyn's talent for self-parody.

Dear Jack,

I was delighted to read in *The Times* that Thomas had received your consent to his engagement. I can confirm the results of your genealogical inquiries. Margaret was at a party in London lately of *ancien régime* Russians who were inquiring anxiously about Thomas's antecedents. His fiancée is plainly 'bien'.

We wish you and Frankie would come here one day before winter sets in. I have some very fine white Bordeaux.

Love to Frankie and congratulations on Thomas's coup.

Evelyn

One of the great trials of Evelyn's life was that he could not persuade Laura to adopt his own meticulous ideas on manners; the spirit was willing but the flesh was very weak indeed, particularly when it came to letter-writing. It was very common when they were at Piers Court on entering the drawing-room to find Laura at a table pen in hand while Evelyn stood over her dictating some letter he had been unable to persuade her to write of her own accord. In 1963 we received a series of postcards from Combe Florey undated by the writer but carrying a postmark.

The first:

Postmark 9.6.63.

Evelyn and I are delighted to learn that you and Jack escaped the massacre of socialists in Salonika, even if it meant your deserting Jack McD.* We greatly look forward to your arrival here on my birthday, June 20th, and to your staying until the morning of Saturday

* Jack McDougall, a director of Chapman and Hall, Evelyn's publishers.

22nd. Or did we arrange other dates? My memory fails.

OXO Laura

Evelyn is much distressed to read of Lord Buckinghamshire's condition.

The only thing that is odd about this post-card is that it was written by Evelyn. It was followed by two others, both in his handwriting.

Postmark 11.6.63.

We are disappointed by the postponement of your visit but appreciate the cogency of your reasons. Please come when you can for as long as you can.

Laura

And:

Postmark 16.6.63.

OXO is a military epigraph – comparable to SWALK & I.T.A.L.Y. – familiar to officers who censored their men's letters. My husband is surprised to learn that it is not employed by sappers.

Laura

In *Men at Arms* SWALK is said to mean SEALED WITH A LOVING KISS. OXO and I.T.A.L.Y. remain to us a mystery.

A postcard carrying the postmark 28.6.60 is in answer to congratulations on a television interview.

Thanks awfully for your card. The BBC people were very silly but civil. Over 30 men were employed in recording that conversation. One of them had been in the party who came to Stinkers and set Pinfold on the run. I asked what had become of the questioner. He has become a professional hypnotist. Significant? Now Diana Oldrich's Box is under investigation in the courts as perhaps you have seen. I hear of you from Mrs Fleming. Meg Dalhousie used to have the King Kong death song played at Government House Salisbury to clear her dinner parties.

E.

Stinkers is the name he gave to Piers Court, Stinchcombe The reference to King Kong is caused by Jack's interest in the South African Music and Drama School responsible for the production of King Kong in London.

And in 1964 a letter:

12 November 64.

Dear Frankie,

I have it on record that you and Jack visit us on 17th. We look forward eagerly to seeing you both. Jack, I understand, lectures to fowl at Torquay – 17th or 19th?

How long will you stay? The longer the better but I should like to know what arrangements to make.

You must be almost the only socialist who is not in the government. Why?

It is very good news that Frank is not at the Home Office. We should all be murdered by sexual maniacs if he were.

Yours ever

Evelyn

Attached to this letter there is a cut-out which says in heavy print: PLEASE STATE WHETHER YOU WOULD LIKE A HOUSE PARTY ARRANGED FOR YOU.

'Frank' refers to Lord Longford whose interest in prison reform and after-care of prisoners is well-known.

But the most typical and I think the most charming letters I received from Evelyn were in acknowledgement of advance copies of books about to be published. I have thought much as to whether I should give them here since they are written to praise my work, but Evelyn so mixed professional appreciation with odd little remarks about everyday life that the effect is spoiled by cutting. I therefore give them in full – the only cuts being of remarks which might offend other people. The first two letters relate to my biography of my father *Freddy Lonsdale*.

Combe Florey House.
January 28th.

Dearest Frankie,

Your book came today. Laura snatched it from me. I fear she may not write at once, so I write now to thank you from us both for giving us this sneak preview. When I have read it I will write again expatiating on its excellencies. . . .

We are glad that neither Teresa or Rose are in jug in Budapest. But perhaps Teresa is. We have not heard from her for some time.

I escape rather often to London and search Brooks's for Jack but without a glimpse. We still suffer awful discomfort – workmen everywhere. Laura collects servants as a dog collects fleas – two indoor men and two and a half women but all they do is make tea for the plumbers. I have been buying objects of art with profligate energy. Do come and see us soon.

Love Evelyn

The paragraph about Teresa and Rose refers to our daughters who had been prevented by their parents from travelling to Hungary at the time of the revolution. Judith Cripps and other undergraduates, who had gone there were, at the time he wrote, in 'jug'.

Combe Florey House
30 January 1957

Dearest Frankie,

I have read your biography with delight and congratulate you with all my heart. Perhaps it is not entirely tactful to say that I am also greatly surprised – surprised that your father had such a fascinating life and that you have the professional skill to handle the material in such a masterly way. Except for a few dozen grammatical slips . . . I don't see how it could be better done. Do you want notes on the slips for future editions or are you sick of revision?

I think you rather overstate your case for the wealth of the '20s. It was much smaller than in the preceding 60 years – numbers of servants, steam yachts, and especially the *plurality* of private houses kept in full commission, never recovered from 1914.

No apology is needed for the aristocracy.

But where you excel is in the most delicate and complex task – of giving a frank and lively and lovable portrait.

What a plain child you were! No nymphet at least not from the photographs you choose.

Love to Jack,

Evelyn.

The second book I sent him was called *Child of the Twenties*, an attempt to give an impression of that period written autobiographically. In it I tried to show why I, like so many other people, became both a Socialist and a member of the Popular Front and in doing this I also discussed the difficulty my generation found in accepting the Christian faith. I was nervous of sending the book to Evelyn as I feared these passages might arouse his wrath. In discussing my antecedents, I remarked that my mother was apt to take undue pleasure in the fact that she was descended from Robert Brooke, a one-time Governor of St Helena.

6th June, 1959.

Dearest Frankie,

It was awfully nice of you to send us your book. We shall treasure it as a pledge of enduring friendship. Your father schooled you well not to be a bore. It is wonderfully readable. In fact I read it at a sitting yesterday. The *Observer* asked me to review it. I have had to return it because, as I told them, it needs someone more familiar with your early milieu and more sympathetic with your conclusions to do it justice. I greatly admired both the matter and the manner of your passages about horses.

Robert Brooke, your ancestor, of the East India Company was the younger son of a younger son ot Brooke of Rantavan (*large* landed proprietors) but I don't think it correct to speak of him as a landed proprietor. He embezzled the Company's funds when collector of taxes at Corah and set up a linen industry in Co. Kildare with the proceeds, which he inaptly named 'Prosperous'. It came a cropper and he tried unsuccessfully to get back his military rank from the Company who sent him instead to St Helena which then (1780) was the dimmest and least lucrative post in their gift. He ruined his brothers in his bankruptcy. He married a widow née Mapletoft. But your mother was quite right in thinking him a gentleman by birth. I thought your references to him lacking in *pietas*. When I say 'embezzled', I merely mean he took the usual rake off.

Do come and see us soon in your fast car. I was in London for two nights last week pretty tight all the time and met lots of chums but not, alas, Jack.

Laura is very much overworked today. The cook has taken to her (the cook's) bed and she (Laura) has been poaching eggs from 7.15 a.m. until now 9.15 with only the help of two gardeners, a cow man and the village woman.

Did you ever know G.R. Margaret is growing exactly like him. Can it be the drink?

Yours ever affec.

Evelyn

Is this a chestnut: The Turkish Ambassador when asked about *Lolita* said, 'In my country we do not like to read of such things. We prefer to see them'?

The third book I sent him was *The Marconi Scandal.* He had been directly responsible for this book having been written. One night at Piers Court Jack made some reference to Herbert Samuel and Evelyn interrupted him to describe Samuel as 'a politician who lost his honour in the Marconi Case'. Jack, who knew no more of the case than most people at that time, did not believe that there could be any truth in this remark. He attacked Evelyn for irresponsibility and afterwards made a great effort to find out something about the case. This proved very difficult. Every biography of the period gave a few lines to it, but no historian appeared to have studied it. For several years at intervals Jack said to me, 'I wish you would write a book about the Marconi case', and at length having nothing better to do I went with him to look at the newspapers in the British Museum. When I realized the extravagance of the charges made by the writers in the paper called the *Eye-Witness* when edited by Hilaire Belloc and the *New Witness* when it was taken over by Cecil Chesterton, knowing that these had not been met by actions for libel, I began to believe the case might be worth greater research. Thus I began to write the book.

Evelyn with his famous notice (*See pages 23–4*)

'Gilbert Pinfold's' Victorian wash-hand stand (*See pages 67–8*)

(*opposite*) The Waugh family in the drawing-room at Combe Florey

Evelyn as he was on our last visit

In the meantime Jack had received three communications from Evelyn on the subject – in what order it is not possible to say as they are all undated.

Piers Court

In the watches of the night I thought of the very simple explanation of Blake's ludicrous attempt to exculpate Herbert Samuel. He is the only one of the gang who is still alive.*

Piers Court

I have been far from well but am better. Marconi case would make a good thesis but sources difficult. There was no defence – merely an attempt to silence. Your sympathies need not be divided as you suppose. *All* the *New Witness* party were Liberals, only one a papist. The Tories began to press the case then called off the attack thus confirming Belloc in his belief that party-politics are a game played by the rich to oppress the poor.

This letter is written on paper headed 'The Manor House, Mells, Frome' but is undated.

Dear Jack,

It seems that my memory was wrong, and that you were right. H. Samuel was never gravely implicated in the celtic conspiracy to make money in Marconi shares.

I am sorry I misinformed you.

Yours ever

Evelyn.

* He means that Herbert Samuel is still alive, and he is thinking of the law in relation to libel.

Immediately before the publication of *The Marconi Scandal* my publisher told me that he had met Evelyn's agent who had told him that Evelyn was asking for an opportunity to review the book. But it was too late, the review copies had been sent out earlier than I had sent the presentation copies and, as the case was of interest to historians, all the papers had already made arrangements. This was a great disappointment to me. Here is the letter he wrote me.

4th August 62.

Dear Frankie,

I have now read *Marconi* with the utmost enjoyment and admiration. You marshal your facts like a trained advocate and lightly carry the huge weight of your research. It must have been a very difficult book to write. You have succeeded beyond expectation. It will get a lot of notice and sell among the middle-aged who are the only people who buy books.

Mrs Cecil Chesterton was a bitch and a liar. I think you inoffensively make that clear. Surely you are mistaken in dating the marriage 'during the Marconi case'? I thought she held him off until she saw him in uniform.

Randolph (for what that is worth) claims it was Sir Winston's idea to gag Carson and Smith by briefing them.

You underrate G. K. Chesterton's achievement and influence. He is not to be judged as a great artist but compared with his peers, Wells and Shaw, he reads fresher today than they. Have you ever read his reply to Wells's History of the World, '*The Everlasting Man*'? Excellent.

Your tenderness towards the Isaacses touches at times on the sloppy. They were, except Rufus who had abilities, incompetent in their own base affairs. One can read this in your quotations but your own picture of Godfrey and Harry as happy-go-lucky good fellows won't wash.

One of the reasons people got so excited about the case was the sanctimonious public aims of the Liberals. From Wolsey to Melbourne no minister was expected to be disinterested. F. E. Smith was frankly and outrageously cynical. But the Liberals were put into power by the nonconformists. No cabinet in its private lives can have been less representative of its supporters.

I wonder how many of the present generation know who Gehazi was.

Yours ever
Evelyn

Chapter 8

A LAST VISIT

WE had arranged to spend two nights at Combe Florey, travelling down by car from London. It was known that Evelyn was himself in London that day, lunching with Pam Berry, and before leaving we went to lunch with Anne Fleming.

This was a good double for two reasons – the first that both Pam and Anne were friends of Evelyn's and also of ours, the second that it is not extravagant to say that together they may be regarded as all that is left of a long tradition of London hostesses. They both entertain in small houses and in a small way compared even with their predecessors of the 1920s, but they both revel in good conversation and exercise much ingenuity and discrimination in providing the environment for it.

Lady Pamela Berry is the daughter of the first Lord Birkenhead and the wife of Michael Berry, proprietor of the *Daily Telegraph* and the *Sunday Telegraph*. When we moved from Gloucestershire to Buckinghamshire she became, if only at weekends, a near neighbour of ours. The first letter that Evelyn wrote to our new home was addressed to us at:

A LAST VISIT

Steeple Claydon
Near Pamberry
Buckinghamshire.

Anne, before she married Ian Fleming, was for many years Lady Rothermere; also the wife of a newspaper proprietor. In the latter years of Evelyn's life she held a very special place in his affections. On his increasingly rare visits to London he nearly always dined with her, but, far more important, it was in writing letters to her, to Nancy Mitford and to Lady Diana Cooper that he whiled away so many hours of his long mornings. As the close friend of so many writers, artists and politicians, Anne was in an exceptional position to provide him with the news and she has in addition an unusual talent for letter-writing. Somerset Maugham once described her as 'the Madame Sévigné of our day', and, when the comparatively few letters and journals of this telephone age are published, hers will almost certainly find a place among the sources available to social historians.

On this particular day Evelyn was lunching with Pam to meet Nigel Dennis whose novel *Cards of Identity* he had greatly admired and who had lately reviewed a book of his for the *Sunday Telegraph*. The night before he had dined with Anne, taking with him his daughter Margaret, but recently of an age to accompany him. When we arrived for luncheon Anne was still suffering from the effects of the evening before. She said she had been very busy and over-tired and she had failed to get a dinner party together and the three of them had dined alone. The evening, she said, had not been a success.

When later that day we drove up the hill to Combe Florey the rear lights of the car that had met Evelyn at the station could be seen in front of us. He was in the hall when we arrived, cold and tired from the journey. As we moved into the sitting-room he asked Laura to bring up a bottle of champagne, but he said that he would himself prefer to bath and change before drinking it. As he left the room he stopped at the door and told us an unpublishable piece of gossip. He opened the door and shut it behind him. Then he opened it again and told us another. This was simply the ritual, but it announced that he was in a good humour.

The champagne we drank before dinner was a pink *Veuve Clicquot* of a famous year which he had been given in return for a service rendered. The owner of the firm had written a short history of the vineyard.

'Not having Frankie's prose style,' he teased in reference to a pleasant remark Pam had made which he had just repeated to me, 'she wished it translated into more elegant English. I performed the service in return for wine. But this was a little extra present.'

The visit to Combe Florey took place very soon after the publication of *Unconditional Surrender* in 1961. At dinner that night Evelyn spoke of Cyril Connolly, saying that he had received a letter from him.

'What did he say of your book?' I asked.

Evelyn had a long-standing relationship with Mr Connolly which I would not presume to discuss except to say that, at the vantage point from which I observed it, the elements of friendship and admiration seemed never entirely missing and often predominant. As critic Mr Connolly stood alone. He made a study of Evelyn's work, and as book after book appeared he reviewed each with increasing authority and much praise. Then on the appearance of the second volume of the war trilogy, *Officers and Gentlemen*, he unexpectedly wrote critically, accusing the novelist of suffering from a 'benign lethargy' and in effect of having written a dull book.

Evelyn, like many another writer, always said that he seldom read the reviews of his books. 'The good ones,' he said, 'give me no pleasure and the bad ones cause me pain.' We all knew that he would read Mr Connolly's review, however, and we expected him to mind about it. On the Sunday it appeared Jack said to me:

'Evelyn will be upset about this. I think we should ask him to dinner to cheer him up.'

'Jack,' I replied, 'I can't ask Evelyn to dinner because Connolly has given him a bad review.'

But Jack persisted and telephoned to Laura who said that Evelyn was away for the day, but was coming back and would probably like to dine with us on his way home.

She sent him a message and Evelyn, who had spent the day in the company of some of the people he loved best in the world, presently arrived in highest good humour. Throughout dinner he was in his gayest mood, and the only reference he made to his book was when Jack congratulated him on it.

'Connolly didn't like it,' he said on an unaccented monotone pitched high, as one stating a fact.

Several months after this he was going away to stay a few weeks in a hotel at Bournemouth, or Folkestone perhaps, and he said before leaving that Cyril Connolly would be staying there too. He suggested he should make it an unpleasant visit for Mr Connolly, and, acting the part of a man with a stick or rolled-up umbrella, he thumped the imaginary back of someone being driven in front of him.

'Be-*nign leth*-argy,' he said, thumping to the rhythm of the words.

But when he came home he said Mr Connolly had not been there. These were the only references he ever made to the defection of his greatest admirer, but Jack and I were unable to believe that this light-hearted gambolling represented his true feelings.

In *Unconditional Surrender*, the third of the trilogy, there is a character named Everard Spruce who seemed to everyone familiar with this world to have certain characteristics reminiscent of Cyril Connolly. The editor of a wartime magazine called *Survival*, Spruce is treated satirically and a little mischievously. But there is no evidence of any feeling of malice and Evelyn seemed, quite good-humouredly, to have got his own back. There is also another character called Ludovic, a mad murderer who writes meaningless *Pensées* which are published by Spruce in *Survival* and received with immoderate acclaim.

Consequently, it was with more than ordinary interest that I asked Evelyn what Mr Connolly had said of this book.

'Well,' he replied, 'you see, Mrs Fleming had made this trouble between us.'

'*Mrs Fleming had?*'

'Yes. She told him the character named Everard Spruce was based on him.'

'*Mrs Fleming did?*'

He explained that on receiving a presentation copy Cyril Connolly had telephoned to Mrs Fleming and, saying he supposed she had also received one, asked her if she would read it over the weekend and allow him to come and see her. Evelyn then signalled Mrs Fleming's agreement with a fluttering of his hands to indicate great excitement. On the Monday Mr Connolly paid the promised call and asked Anne if she thought the character called Spruce could be said to be based on him.

'This put Mrs Fleming on her mettle,' Evelyn said, 'and she replied, "O! yes indeed. And Ludovic too".'

Evelyn said when he had heard of this mischief-making he had written to Cyril and said he hoped that, being himself an imaginative artist, he would know that this was not the way characters are drawn, and he would not allow himself to be put out. Cyril replied that he, of course, quite understood and believed what Evelyn said, particularly as the character bore so little resemblance to himself. Unfortunately, he had added, this is not how the public thinks. They do not say Everard Spruce cannot be Cyril because Cyril is always so well-dressed and gives such marvellous parties. They say, it must be Cyril because he always has such awful clothes, and don't you remember how terrible those parties were that he used to give. Nevertheless, he had written to Evelyn at length about other things and had asked him to his house. Evelyn seemed very much pleased with himself.

However, that night he was angry with 'Mrs Fleming'. Anne, as I have already said, is one of the few people he really loved, whose company never failed to please him. Normally one was hardly allowed to speak of her, certainly not critically. But he had been disappointed the night before. He explained with a sigh that always until recently when he dined with her he had taken her to a restaurant. Now that little Margaret had grown up and accompanied him, he could no longer afford to do this because of her enormous appetite for all the most expensive dishes on the menu. He had thought that Anne would give a little dinner party, choosing with care among his friends to amuse him, and he was genuinely hurt that she had failed to do so.

'But you wrote her a postcard,' I reminded him, 'saying "No riff-raff".'

'Of course not riff-raff,' he replied, 'Mrs Fleming knows plenty of nice people; she could easily have invited some of them. She kept asking me whether I liked the Donaldsons. "Do you like them both?" ' he mimicked. ' "Which do you like best?" She only wanted to repeat what I'd said to you the next day at luncheon.'

We expostulated but he ignored us.

'After all,' he said, 'one likes to have these things teased out of one. She bowled a whole over of these beastly lobs.'

After dinner I said to Laura:

'Evelyn must be very angry with poor Anne. I thought she was sacred ground like Diana.'

'No one is sacred,' Laura replied. 'But he'll get over it.'

The following morning Laura had to go to the dentist in Taunton and I said I would go with her and look at the shops. After breakfast Evelyn, still in very good humour, announced that he would come too and asked me if I would visit the '*antiquaires*' with him.

The Waughs have always had the most terrible cars, enormous second-hand buses bought by Laura to transport the large Catholic family. Now that the children had mostly grown up and left them, she still used a vast and rumbling vehicle to take garden produce to the shops in Taunton. Travelling with Evelyn in one of these cars was usually very painful, because his sense of the behaviour of a gentleman forced him to give up the only comfortable seat beside Laura, while every other instinct rebelled against taking one of the harder ones. This usually induced a dislike of the person who had precipitated the situation, and anger against Laura for possessing such a car. Today nothing upset his benevolence.

'Does Mrs Jarvis know about Coney and Frankie?' he asked me on the way into Taunton.

In *Unconditional Surrender* the character called Everard Spruce has two secretaries. One is called Frankie, the other is called Coney, the nickname by which Mrs Ralph Jarvis is known to her friends. She is someone of whom I see a great deal – enough for people often to say: 'Coney and Frankie', or 'Frankie and Coney'.

'Oh yes,' I replied to his question, 'I rang her up and told her.'

Evelyn giggled. He said, with perfect relevance, but throwing overboard the idea that it was Mrs Fleming who had made the mischief:

'Coney is a much prettier name than Sonia.'

He pronounced the second name with a long O to rhyme with the first.

When Laura left us in Taunton we went first to a photographer so that he might get a passport photograph and then to his bank. On the way to the bank he stopped in the street.

'Do you know my telephone number?' he asked. I replied that I did.

At the bank he instructed them to expect some money in traveller's cheques which would be sent to them for him.

'When it arrives,' he said, 'will you please telephone a message to ...' He turned to me. 'What is my telephone number?' he asked. And I gave it to the man at the counter.

No one except Laura could say for certain whether, having lived at Combe Florey for six or seven years, he was really without knowledge of his own telephone number. My guess is that if, in some imaginary circumstance, he had been held up on a road by a breakdown and had access to a telephone but not to any means of finding out a number, he would not have spent the night away from home. In all other circumstances he would have made the maximum fuss to find out his number rather than simply give it.

When we left the bank we went first to the Museum to see the Glastonbury bowl. Evelyn had never before seen this bowl but it had special associations for him. His father had been given a silver copy of it by a friend who had taken part in the excavations which discovered it and Evelyn had believed this copy to be unique and an object of interest and value. While in Gloucestershire he had been surprised and very cross to find a similar copy in the house of a neighbour, and it was not until he went to live near Taunton that he discovered to his amusement that an enterprising local jeweller had been turning out these copies by the dozen. He then bought several more and they adorned his house as ashtrays. The original bowl in the Taunton Museum is, if I remember correctly, rather larger than the copies and it is made of bronze.

Then we visited the antique shop. This was owned by a man who was also a jeweller, and one passed through the jeweller's shop and down two steps to the room containing the furniture and *objets d'art*. Evelyn stopped in the shop and politely inquired whether we might view the things, and then trotted on down the steps, while I followed close behind him. As he reached the steps and before he was into the room he displayed the connoisseur's eye, that eye which by training and instinct separates the desirable thing from the others in the room faster than the speed of judgement or thought.

'Ah!' he said. 'There is a very useful object. Something everyone needs in his house.'

He trotted on towards a table in the window of the shop on which there reposed a large, well-preserved and highly-polished turtle. He examined this for some time, remarking on its beauty and the excellence of the shell and the polish. When the owner of the shop appeared, he asked him:

'What is the price of your turtle?'

On being told eight guineas, he sighed. 'I shall have to consult my wife,' he said.

After we had left the shop he said to me:

'Much too expensive. Such a pity. I would have given it to Rose for a wedding present and she would have liked it very much.'

In the end he sent Rose a cheque for twenty guineas.

I think this was the last time but one that we ever saw Evelyn. We went once again to Combe Florey, and he was very kind and very gentle, but the life had already gone.

EPILOGUE

At Evelyn's Memorial Service in Westminster Cathedral the Reverend Philip Caraman, S.J., spoke the panegyric. He dwelled on the word '*fidelis*'. Loyal to his country and his faith, loyal to his business associates, his publisher and his agent. Afterwards five of Evelyn's friends were together for luncheon, people who were very fond of him, and in all gravity and sincerity they queried this word '*fidelis*'. Was it, in spite of all Evelyn's great qualities, a word one would have chosen?

He was, it is known, very generous, he gave much in quiet ways to the poor and to charities. I am inspired by the conversation that day to speak of something I know of him which can be known only to very few people.

Ronald Knox died of cancer and some months before his death he suffered a great operation. Afterwards his friends felt that he should have a change of air, a convalescent period away from home. Not one of the people with whom he lived was free to go with him. Evelyn took him to a hotel in Torquay and stayed there with him for several weeks. At first Laura was with them but later she had to leave because at that time the workmen were still at Combe Florey and had to be supervised. Evelyn stayed on for two or three weeks more.

When one considers how difficult he found it to endure anyone outside his family for more than a few hours, how difficult most of us would find it to leave our own beds and live for weeks in an English hotel caring for an old, sick man, how few of us would if it came to it do it, I think this one action earned him the word '*fidelis*'.

INDEX

INDEX

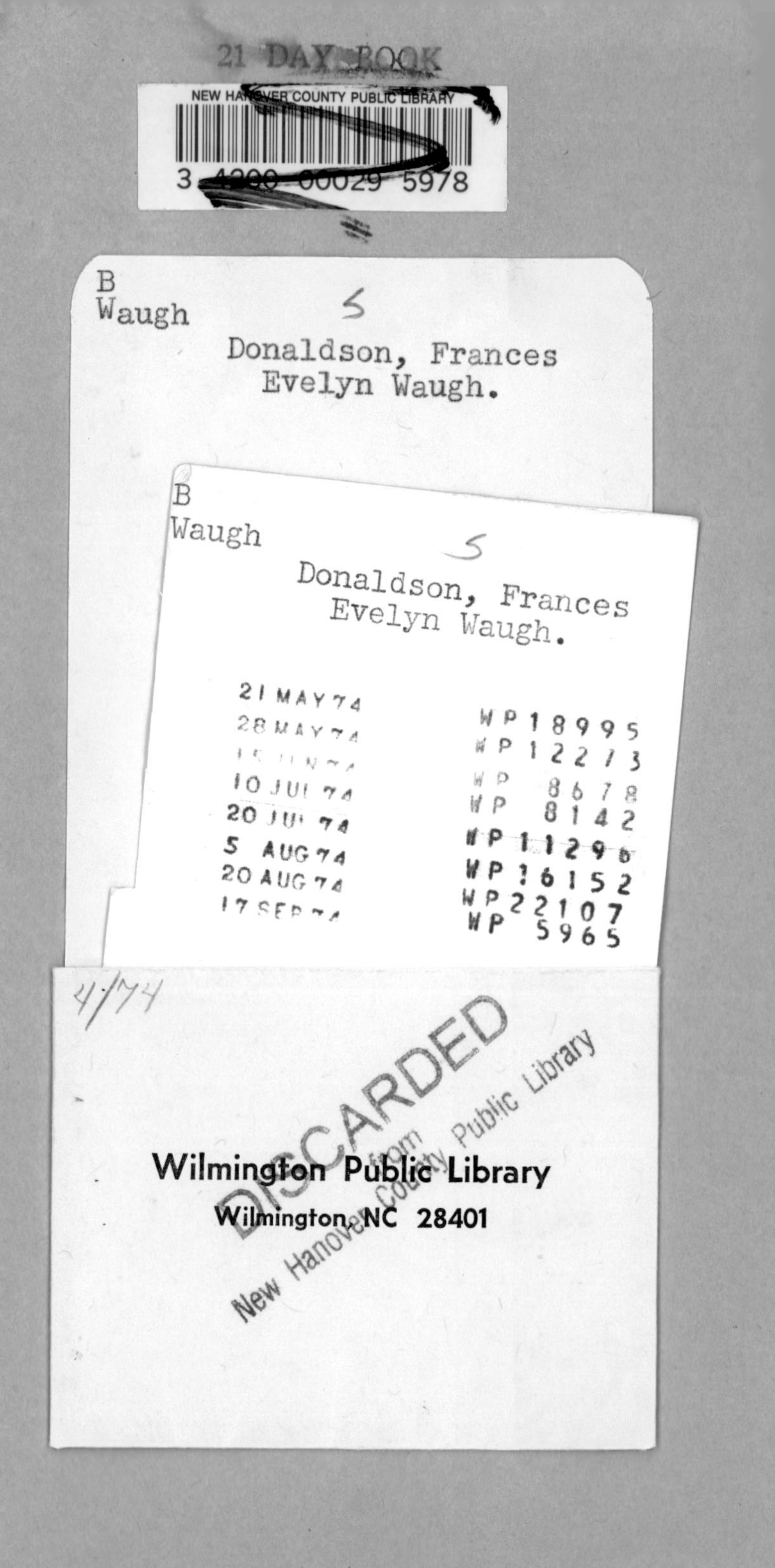
21 DAY BOOK
NEW HANOVER COUNTY PUBLIC LIBRARY
3 4200 00029 5978
B
Waugh
S
Donaldson, Frances
Evelyn Waugh.
B
Waugh
S
Donaldson, Frances
Evelyn Waugh.
21 MAY 74
28 MAY 74
10 JUL 74
5 AUG 74
20 AUG 74
WP 18995
WP 12213
WP 8678
WP 8142
WP 11296
WP 16152
WP 22107
WP 5965
4/74
DISCARDED
from
New Hanover County Public Library
Wilmington Public Library
Wilmington, NC 28401